THE DUAL CERTIFICATION STUDENT TEACHING EXPERIENCE

Billie J. Enz
Arizona State University
Mary Lou Fulton Teachers College

Sally C. Hurwitz
Arizona State University
Mary Lou Fulton Teachers College

B. M. Carlile
Educational Consultant
Phoenix, Arizona

Maureen Gerard
Arizona State University
Mary Lou Fulton Teachers College

Gina Warren
Arizona State University
Mary Lou Fulton Teachers College

Kendall Hunt publishing company

Cover image © Shutterstock

www.kendallhunt.com
Send all inquiries to:
4050 Westmark Drive
Dubuque, IA 52004-1840

CONTENTS

About The Authors

Billie Enz, Ph.D. – Dr. Enz is the author and co-author for several books on new teacher development and mentor training, including: *Trade Secrets: Tips, Tools and Timesavers for Primary and Elementary Teachers;* and *Ready, Set, Teach: A Blueprint for a successful First Year;.* Dr. Enz is a member of the Early Childhood faculty and teaches language and literacy courses.

Sally C. Hurwitz, Ph.D. is Associate Dean in the Mary Lou Fulton Teachers College at Arizona State University at the West campus. She has been in the field of education for over twenty five years, with interest in early childhood education, play, and teacher education. Her current interests focus on the development of beginning teachers, the mentoring process, and staff development.

Barbara J. Carlile, EdD, is an educational consultant in Phoenix, Arizona. She has taught education classes and directs The Teacher Connection, a partnership program for prospective teachers involving the local high schools, community college, and ASU Mary Lou Fulton Teachers College. Dr. Carlile has been involved in education programs at all levels (K–university) in areas such as bilingual education, gifted education, staff development, clinical supervision, cooperative learning, and teacher preparation.

Maureen Gerard, Ph.D. is the Director of the Office of Professional Field Experience at Arizona State University Mary Lou Fulton Teachers College where she directs clinical experiences for pre-service teachers. Her scholarly interests include research in effective teacher preparation, early childhood education and emergent literacy practices. She has published in the areas of family involvement in the early childhood classroom, using environmental print as a literacy tool, and reader's theater for early reading fluency.

Gina Warren, Ed.D is the program coordinator for special education professional development schools. She directs clinical experiences for students in the downtown program at the Mary Lou Fulton Teachers College. Her background in teaching is in K-12 special education. Her research interests are in communities of practice and supporting the professional growth of in-service teachers.

Acknowledgements

The authors wish to thank the following individuals for their contributions to this work

Jody Alexander	Rhea Kowitz	Elaine Reuben
Ceri Alhborn	Billie Laird	Debbie Robinson
Pam Clark	Teena Lugo-Flesher	Elissa Rose
Daisha Oshiro	Edward Murphy	Mary Jo Stegge
Becki Chapman	Teresa Panneton	Cecilia Szymanski
Laura Cohen-Hogan	Traci Peterson	Karen Timberlake
Pam Gaston	Joe Rega	Anne Weissman
Bev Ihinger	Dianne Renne	Elaine Whissen

A note of gratitude to Patsy Arndt for her effort in preparing the text.

A special thank you to Monique Davis for research support.

A special thank you and recognition of the talents of the illustrators:

Brenda Braun, Casey Cook and Chrys Gakopoulos

The authors also wish to thank their families for their understanding and support.

Chapter 1

The Dual Certification Student Teaching Experience

Learning how to teach is a developmental process. However, development is not automatic. Instead, student teachers need many classroom interactions, time to practice, and time for thoughtful reflection. Likewise, development does not occur in isolation. There are many concerned professionals who contribute to a new teacher's education. Through excellent modeling and careful coaching, professors, school principals, mentor teachers, and university supervisors offer student teachers their expertise and diverse experience.

The purpose of this text is to provide explicit information about the ever-evolving roles and responsibilities of the student teaching triad— mentor teacher, student teacher, and university supervisor — at both the prekindergarten and elementary levels. .

The two student teaching experiences provides an exceptional opportunity for student teachers and veteran teachers to work and learn together. All members of the student teaching triad can solve problems, construct new understandings and knowledge about teaching, and develop lasting relationships.

Welcome to student teaching!

University and Public School Collaboration

Coordinator of the Field Experience Office – Before any student teacher enters a school to work with a mentor, a network of professional relationships has been forged between the university and public schools. The Coordinator of Field Experience is a liaison between the university and school districts, and an advocate for preservice teachers. In addition, the coordinator

> ➤ conducts research activities and collaborates with professional peers to continue to improve teacher preparation programs.
> ➤ supervises the placement of student teachers.
> ➤ arranges for the training of mentor teachers through the Mentoring Matters course and
> ➤ hires and prepares university supervisors who are responsible for supporting student teachers through the student teaching semester.

The Principal—The principal is the ultimate voice in the long process of "matching" a student teacher with a veteran teacher. Since the mentor teacher has such a profound effect on a student teacher's professional development, the selection of a veteran to serve as mentor is critical to the success of the student teaching apprenticeship. Obviously, the principal, serving as instructional leader, building manager, community facilitator, and certified evaluator, has the broadest view of the school. Therefore, the principal is charged with helping to identify experienced teachers, at both the prekindergarten and elementary levels, who are willing and able to function as instructional guide, professional advisor, professional confidante, and clinical supervisor to a preservice teacher. Specifically, the principal looks for individuals who demonstrate the following qualities:

> **Instructional Guide.** The mentor teacher should
> ➤ demonstrate excellence in teaching as documented by district evaluations-
> ➤ maintain a positive classroom environment characterized by positive interpersonal skills and proactive management- and
> ➤ structure an exceptional instructional program that features:
>   - initial planning-
>   - comprehensive delivery-
>   - ongoing and summative evaluation of students- and
>   - adjustment of curriculum materials and instructional methods to meet student needs.

> **Professional Advisor.** The mentor teacher is
> ➤ willing to guide a student teacher's professional development,
> ➤ certified in the area in which the student teacher is seeking certification,
> ➤ employed as a full-time teacher during the student teacher's term, and
> ➤ experienced— a minimum of three years of teaching is required in the area of emphasis in which the student teacher is seeking certification.

Personal Confidante. The mentor teacher should
- view sponsorship of a student teacher as a contribution to the profession,
- demonstrate flexibility and a willingness to share classroom responsibility,
- possess a positive and caring personality, and
- demonstrate an ability to work with adults.

Clinical Supervisor. The mentor teacher is
- able to objectively assess the student teacher's instructional performance,
- willing to provide frequent, specific performance feedback,
- able to help the student teacher become a reflective practitioner, and
- able to devote sufficient time to guide the professional growth of a student teacher.

Policy on Substituting:

As the person most responsible for the management of the school, the principal also agrees to respect and protect the parameters of the student teaching apprenticeship. Student teachers need sustained time to develop classroom management and instructional strategies; therefore, they are **not** allowed to serve as substitute teachers during their apprenticeship. Further, while student teachers are expected to assume the mentor teacher's duties, they should not be required to attend to extraordinary or long-term duties not required of the mentor teacher.

The Triad: Roles and Responsibilities

The special education student teacher will have two student teaching apprenticeships; One in a K-12 special education setting and one K-6 general education setting. That means the special education student teacher will work with two different mentor teachers. In both situations the special education student teacher will have a mentor and university supervisor. This triad will work closely together throughout the course of each student teaching experience. The mentor's and supervisor's professional synergy will help the student teacher develop effective instruction strategies and management techniques, as well as the ability to thoughtfully reflect upon practice.

The Mentor Teacher – In both teaching environments; the special education and the general education classroom, the mentor's primary task is to assist the student teacher in understanding and assuming the role of a classroom teacher. The mentor accomplishes this task by modeling, offering explicit verbal explanations, and by providing ongoing, specific, developmentally appropriate performance feedback. If the relationship between mentor teacher and student teacher is built on mutual respect and trust, then the student teacher will actively solicit advice and implement suggestions. Student teachers who continually seek new and better ways to teach will rapidly mature as professional teachers.

This model provides a visual representation of the mentor teacher's multiple roles and responsibilities. Notice that the mentor teacher not only serves as professional advisor, instructional guide, and personal confidante, but also functions as a clinical supervisor. For more information about the mentor's role, see the companion text, *Coaching the Special Education Student Teacher (Dual Certification).* The student teacher will give each mentor one of these texts.

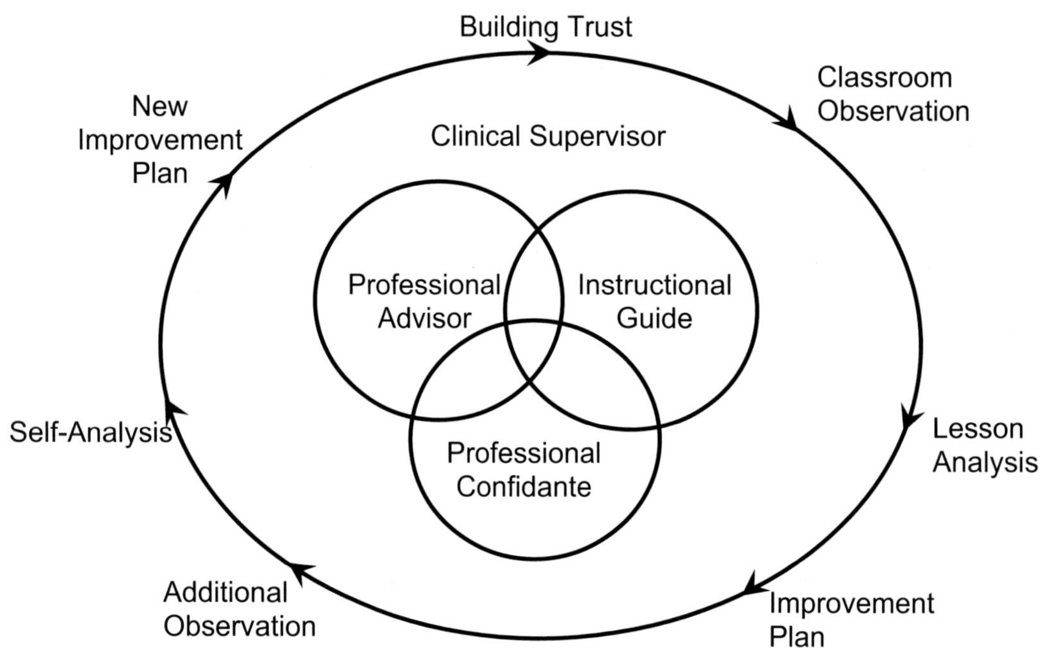

The University Supervisor—The role of the university supervisor is vital to maintaining a high-quality student teaching program. As a liaison representing the University and the Office of Professional Field Experiences, the university supervisor will observe, evaluate and confer with each mentor and student teacher team in both instructional settings. The supervisor provides ongoing support to both mentor and student teacher, and encourages each team to develop the optimum working relationship.

Specific Responsibilities.

Interacts with Mentor Teacher — Initially, the supervisor reviews and clarifies student teaching requirements and expectations. To facilitate communication between triad members, the supervisor will exchange telephone numbers (and/or e-mail addresses) with the mentor. During visits/observations the supervisor will ask the mentor for input about the student teacher's progress. The supervisor is also responsive to the needs and concerns of the mentor teacher (particularly first-time mentors). Finally, the supervisor offers to help the mentor teacher compose the summary narrative and complete the final evaluation.[1]

Builds a Positive Relationship — Supervisors are sensitive to the needs and concerns of the student teacher and provide support and encouragement. The supervisor reviews and clarifies student teaching requirements and expectations. Supervisors open lines of communication with the student teacher by exchanging phone numbers and/or e-mail addresses. Throughout the apprenticeship, supervisors provide guidance and feedback to student teachers about lesson plans, classroom interactions, instructional delivery, notebook reflection entries, resumes, district applications, portfolios, and philosophy statements.

Observes Student Teacher — The supervisor visits/observes the student teacher at least five times during the student teaching experience. After each observation, the university supervisor provides specific, objective feedback. More observations may be required if the student teacher is experiencing difficulty. During the observation the supervisor will

> ➢ review and assess lesson plans, weekly reflection entries, time card and notebook;
> ➢ observe and document the actual 30 to 60 minute lesson;
> ➢ review areas of strength and identify an instructional focus; and
> ➢ participate in a three-way conference as frequently as possible.

Conducts Seminars — Supervisors are required to provide two seminars. To help with scheduling, supervisors will announce the time and place for seminars early in the semester. The topics of the seminars depend on the needs of the student teachers.

---

[1] Both the mentor and student teacher evaluate the university supervisor's effectiveness at the end of the semester. (These forms are included in this text and in the Forms section of *Coaching the Special Education Student Teacher (Dual Certification)*.)

The Student Teacher — Over the course of the semester, successful student teachers assume a great deal of responsibility. They will become full-time classroom teachers in positions of leadership and authority in the schools. Likewise, they have equal responsibility to the college for completing a number of student teaching requirements (pages 21-45). What the student teacher does in the first few days of the apprenticeship will set the tone for the entire experience.

Getting Off to a Strong Start

During the introductory meeting with the mentor teacher, student teachers must review the student teaching requirements and give their mentor teacher the companion text, *Coaching the Special Education Student Teacher (Dual Certification)*. Next, the student teacher and mentor need to review the following:

➤ **Student Teaching Events Calendar** — A helpful calendar of student teaching timelines, seminars and other events given to the student teacher at orientation.

➤ **Developmental Planning Chart** — Allows each mentor and student teacher an opportunity to design the optimum teaching schedule. This plan should allow the student teacher a gradual increase of supported/shared teaching to assume a full-time teaching responsibility. Mentor and student teacher should complete the recommended Developmental Planning Chart on pages 7 and 9 after reading *The Three Phases of Student Teaching* on pages 21-23 (8-week) Developmental Planning Chart examples.

➤ **Student Teacher Questionnaire** — If student teachers are new to the school, they will need to become familiar with their professional colleagues and comfortable in their new working environment. The questionnaire on pages 11-14 also serves as a reminder to the veteran teacher of how much the student teacher needs to learn about the school community.

➤ **Observation Guide and Orientation Activities** — During the first week or two of the student teaching apprenticeship, the student teacher needs to focus intensely on all the intricacies of this complex environment. This activity guide will help the student focus on the student's curriculum and instruction, assessment, classroom organization, and student management. (See pages 15-20).

Developmental Planning

Developmental Planning Chart

8-Week Student Teaching

	Week of:	
Orientation / Partial Responsibility	Week 1	
	Week 2	
Partial to Full Responsibility	Week 3	
	Week 4	
		Midphase Evaluation Due
Full Responsibility	Week 5	
	Week 6	
	Week 7	
Phase-out	Week 8	
		Final Evaluation Due

This is an approximate schedule. Slight adjustments may be made to phasing in and out at the discretion of the mentor and university supervisor.

Developmental Planning Chart

8-Week Student Teaching
Example

	Week of:	
Orientation / Partial Responsibility	Week 1	Observes classroom interactions learns students' names.
	Week 2	Handles opening routines/starts literature study, works with small groups.
Partial to Full Responsibility	Week 3	Manages all routines, including transitions, teaches some lessons
	Week 4	Begins to manage all classroom activities, teaches most lessons,

Midphase Assessment Due

Full Responsibility	Week 5	Teaches all lessons – manages all activities and plans centers, works with paraprofessionals.
	Week 6	Continues full-time teaching. Videotapes best lesson.
	Week 7	Continues full-time teaching.
Phase-out	Week 8	Mentor teacher coteaches most lessons. Begins phasing out

Final Evaluation Due

Student Teacher Questionnaire

This questionnaire is designed to help student teachers become familiar w...
school, and community. It should be completed by the student teacher i...
provided during the <u>first week in the classroom.</u>

General School Information

1. What type of community surrounds the school?

2. What is the ethnic/linguistic composition of the students?

3. What is the average class size? Total school population?

4. What percentage of students receives free or reduced lunch?

5. What resources are available (audiovisual aids, maps, library, computers, other technologies, and copiers)?

Procedures and Policies

6.   What is the daily work schedule?

7.   Are copies of the student handbook available? Where would you find one?

8.   Are copies of the calendar of school activities available? Where would you find one?

9.   What extracurricular activities and meetings should be attended?

10.   Is there a school-wide

discipline policy?   ____

____

grading policy?   ____

____

attendance policy?   ____

____

homework policy?   ____

____

resource system?   ____

____

other?   ____

Classroom Information

11. Describe routines and procedures used most frequently in this classroom (e.g. attendance, attention signal, transitions).

12. What content/skills will be taught? What curriculum or textbooks are used? Teacher's guide? Supplemental material?

13. Does the district or school prefer a particular lesson plan format?

14. Are classes grouped/tracked by academic ability?

15. What abilities or unique needs do the students have?

16. What assessment routines or grading systems are used in this class?

17. What is the process for correcting behavior problems?

18. What are the major interests and activities of the students?

19. How frequently are teachers expected to communicate with parents by phone, email, or newsletter?

Personal/Professional Concerns

20.   What is the mentor teacher's professional background?

21.   What is the proper dress for student teachers?

22.   When can daily meetings for lesson planning and informal feedback be held?

23.   List the names of the following personnel:

Administrators	
Secretaries	
Librarians	
Nurses	
Counselors	
Special Education Personnel	
ESL Personnel	
Teachers Aides	
Classroom Volunteers	
Other	

24.   When is the best time for the mentor and the student teacher to discuss the weekly progress forms? (See weekly progress forms in *Coaching the Special Education Student Teacher (Dual Certification)*.)

25.   What might be good times for the university supervisor to schedule observations?

Observation Guide and Orientation Activities

These activities are designed to carefully guide observations during the first phase of the student teaching experience. The mentor can help provide this information

I.   Learning About Your Students

   A.   Describe the student diversity in the classroom (socioeconomic, gender, culture, language, achievement).

   B.   Who are the students in this classroom? How do they vary from one another? How are they alike? What is the impact of student diversity on instruction?

   C.   Visit the counselor or special area teacher to discuss the academic, social, and emotional concerns of students with special needs. What services are provided for these students?

   D.   How do various cultures and the community influence this school/class?

II. Learning About Curriculum and Instructional Presentation

   A. Look through state academic standards and/or district courses of study, curriculum guides, scope and sequence guides. How does this information help or hinder the teacher's planning?

   B. Describe the instructional plans actually used in this classroom. Could a new teacher follow these plans and teach this class?

   C. Observe the mentor teacher implementing a lesson/activity. Describe how the teacher involved students in the learning process, adapted instruction for student diversity, and assessed student understanding.

   D. Describe and analyze the instructional techniques the mentor teacher most often uses.

   E. Observe and describe a discussion involving students. How did the mentor initiate and maintain student involvement?

   F. Review instructional resources in the mentor's classroom. Determine how to access district resources and materials.

III.   Learning About Student Assessment

A.   Describe the mentor teacher's assessment/grading system. Identify the various sources of information used to make decisions about student progress and grades.

B.   Identify and describe achievement/grading standards and/or expectations the district established for assessment.

C.   Describe how the mentor teacher involves the students in self-assessment and grading processes.

D.   How is information about student assessment communicated to parents?

IV. Learning About Classroom Organization and Child Management

    A. Ask the mentor teacher what classroom routines are considered the most critical and why.

    B. Observe and describe several management routines, including:
- Passing out student papers and work.
- Student transitions: such as entering, leaving, moving within the room, and between instructional activities.
- Beginning and ending of school day or class period.
- Sharpening pencils, using restroom, disposing of trash, etc.
- Getting students' attention.
- Giving directions or assignments.
- Food service/snack time

    C. Describe teacher's routines for grading papers, completing required paperwork, and/or performing clerical tasks.

    D. Describe the routines the mentor teacher uses during the first day and/or week of school to establish consistent management and a positive classroom environment.

V. Learning About Student Management

    A.   Observe and describe nonverbal behaviors the mentor teacher uses to monitor/manage students.

    B.   List and describe specific examples of social reinforcers used by the mentor teacher. Note how the students responded.

    C.   Observe and describe the types of intervention the mentor uses to manage inappropriate behavior. What approaches work best?

    D.   Describe any schoolwide/districtwide adopted discipline plans.

V.   Learning About the Classroom Organization and Room Arrangement

A. Draw a diagram of the room. Label all centers (blocks, art, library, home center, dramatic play center, listening center, writing center, science, etc.) student meeting areas, teacher work space, material storage, etc.

B. Make a brief inventory of activities and materials in each of the centers. How did the teacher develop the curriculum/activity in the centers? How are center materials stored? How are center materials maintained?

C. How do the centers work? How long are children in the centers? How do children rotate from center to center? How does the teacher assess children's work in the center?

D. How are aides and/or parent volunteers utilized in this classroom? How does the teacher communicate with aides/parents to discuss classroom lessons, preparation, student's progress?

Chapter 2

The Three Phases of Student Teaching: An Overview

Teaching is an immensely complex, multifaceted endeavor. To maximize a student teacher's chances for success, the mentor teacher must carefully and deliberately develop a plan to gradually increase the student teacher's level of instructional responsibilities. The next three pages review the recommended activities and requirements for each triad member for each phase of the student teaching experience. After the mentor and student teacher review the phases, they should complete the Developmental Planning Chart on page 7 for the 8-week plan.

Regardless of the phase, student teachers are required to be on duty at their assigned school for the complete school day during the entire semester. Complete school day is defined as the duty day for teachers in the building where the assignment is made. For example, if teachers are expected to be on duty from 7:30 a.m. to 3:30 p.m., the same expectations are made for the student teacher. The professional day includes in-service and parent conferences.

CAUTION: The student teaching semester demands, and should receive, full attention. This apprenticeship will require the student to be a full-time teacher. Most student teachers quickly discover that a teacher's day does not end at 4:00 p.m. Instead, the preparation of lesson plans and grading may require continued work far beyond the regular workday. To be successful, the student teacher may need to sharply curtail other employment. The Office of Professional Field Experience requests that the student teacher's time and energy be focused on this demanding but most exciting and rewarding experience.

The Developmental Phases of Student Teaching

To maximize a student teacher's chances for success, the mentor teacher needs to carefully and deliberately create a plan that gradually increases the student teacher's level of instructional responsibility to match the student teacher's growing knowledge, skill and neuron-networks. This gradual transition is a sensitive and critical process. If student teachers begin to acquire too much responsibility too soon, they often become frustrated, overwhelmed, and consequently lose confidence in their ability to teach. On the other hand, if student teachers are restricted in opportunities to practice and strengthen their knowledge and skill, their development ceases.

The next few pages review the recommended activities for each triad member for each developmental phase of the student teaching experience for eight weeks. After the mentor and student teacher review the phases, they should complete the Developmental Planning Chart on page 23 for an 8-week experience.

PHASE I for 8 Week Student Teaching: Orientation/Assuming Partial Responsibility – Weeks 1-2

Student Teacher	Date
❑ Becomes familiar with colleagues and school facility.	
❑ Learns names of students and becomes familiar with their unique needs.	
❑ Observes instruction using Observation Guide and Orientation Activities. P 9-18	
❑ Observes classroom routines and procedures, describes them in writing. P 9-18	
❑ Participates in classroom routine, i.e. attendance, recording grades.	
❑ Instructs entire class with intense supervision.	
❑ Participates in related activities, i.e. faculty meetings, athletic events.	
❑ Tutors individual students and small groups.	
❑ Becomes familiar with content to be taught later in the 8 week placement.	
❑ Begins to develop detailed unit/daily lesson plans.*	
❑ Begins teaching, following lesson plans prepared by mentor.	
❑ Constructs teaching activities that motivate learning.	
❑ Keeps reflection entries, Blackboard discussions, timecard, notebook up to date.	
❑ Attends university and supervisor seminars.	
Mentor Teacher	
❑ Maintains responsibility for planning and conducting class but involves student teacher in planning; shares long-range plans for 8 week placement.*	
❑ Involves student teacher in routine procedures, preparation of materials, and interaction with students.	
❑ Reinforces standards for initial lesson planning.*	
❑ Set aside a special time each day to review student teacher questions.	
❑ Provides specific feedback to student teacher frequently. (See Weekly Progress Form in *Coaching the Special Education Student Teacher (Dual Certification)*	
❑ Completes and reviews, with student teacher and university supervisor, the Professional Attributes and Characteristics Scale and Instructional Development Scale at the end of the fifth week. (*See Coaching the Special Education Student Teacher (Dual Certification)*.)	
University Supervisor	
❑ Holds orientation meeting and reviews requirements.	
❑ Determines seminar content based on student teacher concerns, and establishes times and locations for seminars.	
❑ Conducts introductory meeting with mentor and student teacher.	
❑ Observes and confers with student teacher and mentor.	
❑ Reinforces standards for initial lesson planning.*	
❑ Discusses the first trimester evaluation with student teacher and mentor.	

*Initially, lesson plans should be quite detailed. As the student teacher becomes competent in carrying out plans, there may be less written detail. Generally, as the teaching load of the student teacher increases, the amount of detail in lesson plans will decrease and may be written in the teacher's daily plan book.

PHASE II for 8-Week Student Teaching: Partial to Full Responsibility
Weeks 3-4

Student Teacher **	Date
❑ Identifies special class characteristics – relates instruction to students.	
❑ Manages all routine tasks and classroom procedures.	
❑ Gradually assumes full instructional responsibility for the school day as teaching proficiency increases.	
❑ Develops all lesson plans with guidance from mentor teacher, using the format approved by university supervisor	
❑ Continues to develop instructional materials for lessons.	
❑ Participates in faculty meetings, parent/teacher conferences, PTA meetings, and staff development workshops offered through the district.	
❑ Continues to maintain reflection entries, timecard, and notebook.	
❑ Asks mentor teacher and university supervisor for specific feedback on lesson plans, classroom management, and instructional performance.	
❑ Attends seminars and completes other assignments as required by the university supervisor.	
Mentor Teacher	
❑ Plans instruction cooperatively with the student teacher.	
❑ Models a variety of instructional techniques so that student teacher develops a comfort level for a wide range of teaching activities.	
❑ Continuously assesses the student teacher's level of competency in lesson planning, classroom management, and instructional delivery.	
❑ Provides daily feedback to the student teacher.	
❑ Completes and reviews Weekly Progress forms with student teacher.	
❑ Completes and reviews the Professional Attributes and Characteristics Scale and the Instructional Development Scale with the student teacher and university supervisor at midphase.	
University Supervisor	
❑ Conducts one or two observations. Confers with the student teacher/mentor.	
❑ Conducts at least one seminar.	
❑ Confers with student teacher and mentor about second-trimester evaluation.	
❑ Advises and supports mentor and/or student teacher as required.	
❑ Reviews timecard, notebook, weekly reflection entries, and other assignments, as necessary.	

(Adapted from Student Teaching Handbook from the University of Arizona, Beeker and Kroeger, 1991.)

PHASE III - 8-Week Student Teaching: Full Responsibility/Phaseout
Weeks 5-8*

Student Teacher **	Date
❑ Sustains primary responsibility for lesson planning, preparing materials, delivering instruction, and monitoring student progress.	
❑ Implements and maintains an effective guidance plan.	
❑ Communicates with parents (via face-to-face conversations, newsletters, personal notes, phone calls, and/or parent conferences) under mentor's supervision.	
❑ Assumes primary responsibility for student assessment and makes recommendations to mentor teacher.	
❑ Provides instruction that recognizes individual student needs.	
❑ Continues to maintain reflection entries, Blackboard discussion, timecard, and notebook.	
❑ Asks the school principal (or other building administrator, such as grade-level or department chair) to observe a lesson and provide feedback.	
❑ Videotapes "best lesson" for reflection.	
❑ Completes university supervisor's evaluation.	
❑ Attends seminar and completes other assignments as required by the university supervisor.	
Mentor Teacher	
❑ Examines, critiques, and approves student teacher's plans for instruction and student assessment.	
❑ Assumes primary responsibility for pupils' final grades.	
❑ Continues to observe and assess the student teacher's instruction.	
❑ Provides daily feedback to the student teacher.	
❑ Occasionally models instructional strategies.	
❑ Completes and reviews Weekly Progress forms with student teacher.	
❑ Completes summative evaluation	
❑ Completes university supervisor's evaluation.	
University Supervisor	
❑ Conducts one observation. Confers with the student teacher/mentor.	
❑ Conducts at least one seminar.	
❑ Confers with student teacher and mentor about summative evaluation.	
❑ Advises and supports mentor and/or student teacher as required.	
❑ Reviews timecard, notebook, weekly reflection entries, and other assignments, as necessary.	

* Final week - Gradual phaseout (mentor teacher should approve any outside observations).

**Special Education and Elementary student teachers will assume the full teaching responsibilities of the mentor teacher. Some exceptions may apply. If so, please speak to the supervisor. (Adapted from Student Teaching Handbook from the University of Arizona, Beeker and Kroeger, 1991.)

Special Note:

Special education student teachers should
>attend and, if possible, lead an Individualized Education Program (IEP) meeting,
>attend and, if possible, lead a parent/teacher conference, and
>facilitate naming/writing Individualized Education Programs (IEP) goals.

Special Education student teachers should also
>experience a disciplinary action,
>experience writing Functional Behavior Analysis (FBA), if possible
>understand schools/districts' referral process, and
>experience the multiple roles of a special education teacher.

Special education student teacher lessons plans should
>cross-reference standards with Individualized Education Program goals,
>accommodate/modify lesson plans to reflect academic and behavior objectives, and
>provide differentiated instruction.

The intensity of the student teaching semester will help prepare student teachers for their first year in the classroom.

Chapter 3

Student Teaching Requirement

All student teachers are required to
  - ➤ write weekly reflections,
  - ➤ participate in Blackboard discussion groups,
  - ➤ maintain an accurate timecard,
  - ➤ organize instructional information in a notebook,
  - ➤ attend professional seminars, and
  - ➤ tape themselves teaching a lesson.

The university supervisor will assess these basic requirements each time the student teacher is observed. The following section provides specific information about student teaching requirements and how each requirement is assessed.

Student teaching will test your organizational skills.

Professional Seminars

Student teaching seminars are designed in part to provide student teachers with the opportunity to share personal experiences and ideas with one another in a supportive, nurturing environment. The university supervisor and the Office of Professional Field Experience determine the content, locations and times for the seminars. Student teachers are required to attend five professional seminars by the end of the student teaching experience. . University supervisors provide **two** seminars. The content of the seminars varies from one university supervisor to another, depending on the specific concerns of the student teachers. Seminars might include topics such as management and discipline strategies, classroom organization techniques, and specific instructional skills.

Career Services offers **two** possible student teaching seminars.
> Job Search Strategies – Student teachers will learn the necessary skills to search for their first teaching position.
> Successful Interviewing – This seminar will be embedded in your capstone course. If your program does not require a capstone course, please review your student teacher events calendar for the dates and times this seminar will be offered.

Mary Lou Fulton Teachers College

Seminars: All students are required to attend three seminars of their choice. Seminars, dates, and times are listed in your events calendar.

NOTE: Attendance at seminars will be recorded on the
Student Teaching Timecard. This time can be recorded
as related activities.

Weekly Reflection Entry

The weekly reflection entry serves several purposes. First, it allows student teachers an opportunity to analyze their developing practice deeply and thoughtfully. Second, it offers the university supervisor a unique way to "see" the student teacher's thinking. Each week the student teacher will describe a classroom event and the event's impact on the student teacher.

The weekly reflection entries are read <u>only</u> by the university supervisor. The examples on pages 30–31 illustrate the types of concerns that may be discussed through the weekly reflection entry. Remember, these examples are only guides. As each student teacher's classroom experiences are unique, what student teachers choose to write about will be based on their perception of what is important to reflect upon. The weekly reflection entry is typically one to two pages in length and is organized into four parts.

1.   Describe an event that occurred in your classroom this week.

2.   Provide details about it, such as information about the students, teachers, parents, and administrators who were involved.

3.   What were your feelings and actions?

4.   What did you learn?

Weekly reflection entries contribute to the student teacher grade and are required. They should be timely, appropriately formatted, well written and provide good insight into a classroom event.

Weekly Reflection Entry — Third Grade Example — Week 1

My mentor teacher (MT) explained to me that the first day of school is very important for setting guidelines in your classroom. He stressed procedures, procedures, procedures. He told me that you have to teach your students how you want things done in your classroom so the third-grade students do them correctly. He taught the students different procedures and also had the students write them down in their notes to stress the importance of them. He acknowledged that you will never get in trouble for a procedure, but if it is not done correctly, we will practice it until it is done correctly.

My MT had me teach a procedure to the class so the students got used to seeing me teach in front of the class. I taught a procedure on getting the class' attention. I taught them what I, the teacher, am going to do and what it is going to look and sound like. Then I taught them what they need to do as the student, what they are going to look and sound like. The key word that we are going to use this year is "eyeballs." When I raise my hand and say "eyeballs", the students will freeze, be silent, show me five fingers, and look directly at me. After I taught my students the procedure of how I want to get my students attention, we practiced it. I had a student walk to the pencil sharpener so someone would be out of their seat moving around. I waited a few seconds, then I said "eyeballs" with my hand raised. I made sure the student at the pencil sharpener stopped, gave me five fingers, was silent, and was looking directly at me. Then I proceeded to look at each student to make sure they were doing the correct procedure. At one point, one of my students was not holding up five fingers, so I kept looking at him while I was holding up five fingers. Once he got the procedure right, I continued to scan the rest of the class. Once everyone was doing what they were supposed to be doing, I told my students what a great job they did. I quickly went through the procedure one more time and then we continued with the rest of the day's notes. My MT used the procedure periodically during his lesson so the students would get practice with it.

I never realized how important procedures were to the classroom. They can really help make the classroom run smoothly. If the students are taught correctly and you hold them accountable for their actions, they will do what you ask of them. If the class is ever too rowdy or they are working in groups and I need to get their attention to give them an announcement, I know by teaching them this procedure I will be able to get their attention quickly without having to shout or raise my voice. At first I thought it was silly to have an attention-getting procedure and teach it to my students, but after implementing it I really see why it needs to be done. I feel, as a beginning teacher, having a procedure for getting attention is something that needs to be done to keep an orderly classroom.

I learned that procedures, as simple as this might seem at first, are incredibly important. If I teach my students at the beginning of the year how things are to be done in my classroom, it will greatly help my classroom management. I feel that classroom management is one of the most important skills to have to run an orderly classroom.

Weekly Reflection Entry Example – Week 6

1. Describe an event that occurred in your classroom this week.

Karen is in the 4-year-old class. Recently she has begun clinging to her mother when she is dropped off each day. She has also started crying, usually during times of transition or when not occupied wanting her mother and father. She has started having frequent accidents and refuses to go to the bathroom because she is "afraid something is going to get her". According to the teachers, this behavior started after returning from winter break. Before break she was a happy, independent child who actively participated. She rarely cried and never had accidents.

2. Provide details about the event, such as information about the students, parents, teachers, and administrators who were involved.

It would seem something is going on to cause such a dramatic regression. However, in almost daily meetings with her mother nothing seems amiss. The mother claims she is displaying unusual behavior at home too, frequently crying, and acting jealous towards her younger brother. Nothing has been said about accidents at home. The mother states it's just a phase, yet the teachers feel there is some underlying reason to her behavior. Whether there is a reason or not, trying to find strategies of managing her behavior is difficult.

One thought is that maybe she needs extra attention. The teachers claim that last semester she seemed to be always quiet and on her best behavior and so there wasn't too much personal interaction with her. When she cries or has an accident she gets attention from everyone, the teacher and the other children.

3. What were your feelings and actions during the event?

I feel helpless because I don't know what is going on and I'm not sure what to do. I don't want to make her fears worse. Likewise I don't want to reinforce inappropriate behavior.

4. What did you learn from the event?

I learned that you always need to look into problems and gather as much information as you can in order to help a child. We decided to try giving her praise and attention when she is doing the right thing and helping out, and also interacting with her more during center time. So far it seems to be helping her get the nurturing and attention she needs in a positive way, instead of a negative.

Student Teaching Timecard

Student teachers are **required** to keep a timecard to document the time spent in student teaching activities. The accurate completion and submission of the timecard to the Office of Professional Field Experience will be a partial determinant of the student teacher's grade, as well as one means of determining eligibility for certification.

Time is allocated in one of four categories. Student teachers will need to record the exact amount of time spent for each category. Weekly time sheets are used to record the time on a daily basis (pages 37-44). The categories of student teaching are defined as follows:

> **OBSERVATION** — Time spent observing any and all activities occurring within the school and/or classroom.

> **ACTUAL TEACHING** —Time spent working <u>directly</u> with children, for example whole class, small group, and/or individuals in the classroom, on the field, on the stage, in the gymnasium, etc.

> **PREPARATION** — Time spent preparing to teach. This time includes activities such as researching, previewing, and organizing instructional materials; writing lesson plans; grading; working on instructional displays; and developing instructional materials.

> **RELATED ACTIVITIES** — Time spent in activities such as assemblies; faculty meetings; seminars; extracurricular school events; conferences with the mentor teacher; supervisor; and parents; staff development meetings; professional seminars; etc. A full list of activities is available through your supervisor.

Time spent is allocated to one and only one category. The combined time in observation and actual teaching cannot exceed the total time your students are physically in school. Record the time spent each day in each area on your weekly time sheet. At the end of the week, total your hours, rounding to the nearest whole hour.

Figure 1 is a reproduction of the student teaching timecard which contains spaces for use in recording the amount of time devoted to each of the activities related to teaching. On this timecard, spaces have been provided for a total of 16 weeks. In many cases, student teachers will begin their apprenticeship prior to the official university start date. The hours accumulated prior to student teaching may be totaled and placed in the pre-student teaching column. (This applies to all early start students.) Likewise, some student teachers will wish to stay beyond the university's completion date.

The hours accumulated after the formal student teaching experience may be totaled and placed in the post-student teaching column. Since the timecard is an important document for graduation and certification requirements, care should be taken in completing it.

Figure 1 — Sample Student Teaching Time Card

STUDENT TEACHING TIMECARD   ARIZONA STATE UNIVERSITY   ASU

❑ **Mary Lou Fulton Teachers College**

STUDENT NAME (Last, First, Middle)	ASU I.D. NO.	☐ Fall ☐ Spring Year:

Specialization: ☐ BLE ☐ ECD ☐ EED ☐ ESL ☐ SPE ☐ SE

Course Number: ☐ 478 ☐ 578

Final grade

Local Address (no, Street, Apt.) — Phone

City/State/Zip — Email

Placement Information
District _______________
School _______________
Address _______________
Phone _______________

Mentor Teacher

Supervisor

Grade Level or Subject

	Pre-Student Teaching	REQUIRED WEEKS (Report number of hours spent per activity)																Post-Student Teaching	Total
		1	2	3	4	5	6	7	8	9	10	11	12	13	14	15	16		
Observation																				
Actual Teaching																				
Preparation																				
Related Activities																				
TOTAL NUMBER OF HOURS																				
Mentor Teacher's Initials																				
University Supervisor's Initials																				

I certify that the above information is correct.

STUDENT TEACHER'S SIGNATURE	DATE	COORDINATOR, PROFESSIONAL FIELD EXPERIENCES	DATE

Information must be recorded in ink.

Minimum Hours of Student Teaching Activity	
Type of Activity	8-Week
Observation	60
Actual Teaching	105
Preparation	90
Related Activities	45
TOTAL	**300**

At the end of student teaching, the completed timecard should reflect these minimum clock hours.

The student teacher is responsible for securing the mentor teacher's and university supervisor's initials indicating their agreement with the student teacher's record keeping.

DON'T PANIC!

Although these numbers seem unattainable at first glance, let's take a minute to break down the values. Most student teachers spend between 45 and 60 hours per week (including evening and weekends). This includes observing, teaching, grading papers, attending meetings, preparing lesson plans, etc.

Student teachers need to use the Weekly Time Sheets to track their weekly progress and semester totals on a weekly basis.

The hours will go by quickly…be sure to keep track of your time.

WEEKLY TIME SHEET

Date: _________________   Week #: _________________

Record the number of hours each day for each activity.

Activity	Mon	Tue	Wed	Thu	Fri	Sat/Sun	Activity Total	Hours Used
Observation/ Participation								____ + ____ = ____
Actual Teaching								____ + ____ = ____
Preparation								____ + ____ = ____
Related Activities								____ + ____ = ____
Grand Total								

Student Teacher Initials _________________ Mentor Teacher Initials _________________

WEEKLY TIME SHEET

Date: _________________   Week #: _________________

Record the number of hours each day for each activity.

Activity	Mon	Tue	Wed	Thu	Fri	Sat/Sun	Activity Total	Hours Used
Observation/ Participation								____ + ____ = ____
Actual Teaching								____ + ____ = ____
Preparation								____ + ____ = ____
Related Activities								____ + ____ = ____
Grand Total								

Student Teacher Initials _________________ Mentor Teacher Initials _________________

WEEKLY TIME SHEET

Date: ________________   Week #: ____________________

Record the number of hours each day for each activity.

Activity	Mon	Tue	Wed	Thu	Fri	Sat/Sun	Activity Total	Hours Used
Observation/ Participation								____ + ____ = ____
Actual Teaching								____ + ____ = ____
Preparation								____ + ____ = ____
Related Activities								____ + ____ = ____
Grand Total								

Student Teacher Initials ____________________ Mentor Teacher Initials ____________________

WEEKLY TIME SHEET

Date: ________________   Week #: ____________________

Record the number of hours each day for each activity.

Activity	Mon	Tue	Wed	Thu	Fri	Sat/Sun	Activity Total	Hours Used
Observation/ Participation								____ + ____ = ____
Actual Teaching								____ + ____ = ____
Preparation								____ + ____ = ____
Related Activities								____ + ____ = ____
Grand Total								

Student Teacher Initials ____________________ Mentor Teacher Initials ____________________

WEEKLY TIME SHEET

Date: _________________   Week #: _________________

Record the number of hours each day for each activity.

Activity	Mon	Tue	Wed	Thu	Fri	Sat/Sun	Activity Total	Hours Used
Observation/ Participation								____ + ____ = ____
Actual Teaching								____ + ____ = ____
Preparation								____ + ____ = ____
Related Activities								____ + ____ = ____
Grand Total								

Student Teacher Initials _________________ Mentor Teacher Initials _________________

WEEKLY TIME SHEET

Date: _________________   Week #: _________________

Record the number of hours each day for each activity.

Activity	Mon	Tue	Wed	Thu	Fri	Sat/Sun	Activity Total	Hours Used
Observation/ Participation								____ + ____ = ____
Actual Teaching								____ + ____ = ____
Preparation								____ + ____ = ____
Related Activities								____ + ____ = ____
Grand Total								

Student Teacher Initials _________________ Mentor Teacher Initials _________________

WEEKLY TIME SHEET

Date: _________________   Week #: ___________________

Record the number of hours each day for each activity.

Activity	Mon	Tue	Wed	Thu	Fri	Sat/Sun	Activity Total	Hours Used
Observation/ Participation								____ + ____ = ____
Actual Teaching								____ + ____ = ____
Preparation								____ + ____ = ____
Related Activities								____ + ____ = ____
Grand Total								

Student Teacher Initials ___________________Mentor Teacher Initials ___________________

WEEKLY TIME SHEET

Date: _________________   Week #: ___________________

Record the number of hours each day for each activity.

Activity	Mon	Tue	Wed	Thu	Fri	Sat/Sun	Activity Total	Hours Used
Observation/ Participation								____ + ____ = ____
Actual Teaching								____ + ____ = ____
Preparation								____ + ____ = ____
Related Activities								____ + ____ = ____
Grand Total								

Student Teacher Initials ___________________Mentor Teacher Initials _________________ ______

WEEKLY TIME SHEET

Date: _________________ Week #: __________________

Record the number of hours each day for each activity.

Activity	Mon	Tue	Wed	Thu	Fri	Sat/Sun	Activity Total	Hours Used
Observation/ Participation								____ + ____ = ____
Actual Teaching								____ + ____ = ____
Preparation								____ + ____ = ____
Related Activities								____ + ____ = ____
Grand Total								

Student Teacher Initials _____________________ Mentor Teacher Initials _____________________

WEEKLY TIME SHEET

Date: _________________ Week #: __________________

Record the number of hours each day for each activity.

Activity	Mon	Tue	Wed	Thu	Fri	Sat/Sun	Activity Total	Hours Used
Observation/ Participation								____ + ____ = ____
Actual Teaching								____ + ____ = ____
Preparation								____ + ____ = ____
Related Activities								____ + ____ = ____
Grand Total								

Student Teacher Initials _____________________ Mentor Teacher Initials _____________________

WEEKLY TIME SHEET

Date: ___________________   Week #: ____________________

Record the number of hours each day for each activity.

Activity	Mon	Tue	Wed	Thu	Fri	Sat/Sun	Activity Total	Hours Used
Observation/ Participation								____ + ____ = ____
Actual Teaching								____ + ____ = ____
Preparation								____ + ____ = ____
Related Activities								____ + ____ = ____
Grand Total								

Student Teacher Initials ____________________ Mentor Teacher Initials ____________________

WEEKLY TIME SHEET

Date: ___________________   Week #: ____________________

Record the number of hours each day for each activity.

Activity	Mon	Tue	Wed	Thu	Fri	Sat/Sun	Activity Total	Hours Used
Observation/ Participation								____ + ____ = ____
Actual Teaching								____ + ____ = ____
Preparation								____ + ____ = ____
Related Activities								____ + ____ = ____
Grand Total								

Student Teacher Initials ____________________ Mentor Teacher Initials ____________________

WEEKLY TIME SHEET

Date: _________________   Week #: _________________

Record the number of hours each day for each activity.

Activity	Mon	Tue	Wed	Thu	Fri	Sat/Sun	Activity Total	Hours Used
Observation/ Participation								____ + ____ = ____
Actual Teaching								____ + ____ = ____
Preparation								____ + ____ = ____
Related Activities								____ + ____ = ____
Grand Total								

Student Teacher Initials _________________ Mentor Teacher Initials _________________

WEEKLY TIME SHEET

Date: _________________   Week #: _________________

Record the number of hours each day for each activity.

Activity	Mon	Tue	Wed	Thu	Fri	Sat/Sun	Activity Total	Hours Used
Observation/ Participation								____ + ____ = ____
Actual Teaching								____ + ____ = ____
Preparation								____ + ____ = ____
Related Activities								____ + ____ = ____
Grand Total								

Student Teacher Initials _________________ Mentor Teacher Initials _________________

WEEKLY TIME SHEET

Date: _________________   Week #: __________________

Record the number of hours each day for each activity.

Activity	Mon	Tue	Wed	Thu	Fri	Sat/Sun	Activity Total	Hours Used
Observation/ Participation								____ + ____ = ____
Actual Teaching								____ + ____ = ____
Preparation								____ + ____ = ____
Related Activities								____ + ____ = ____
Grand Total								

Student Teacher Initials ___________________ Mentor Teacher Initials ___________________

WEEKLY TIME SHEET

Date: _________________   Week #: __________________

Record the number of hours each day for each activity.

Activity	Mon	Tue	Wed	Thu	Fri	Sat/Sun	Activity Total	Hours Used
Observation/ Participation								____ + ____ = ____
Actual Teaching								____ + ____ = ____
Preparation								____ + ____ = ____
Related Activities								____ + ____ = ____
Grand Total								

Student Teacher Initials ___________________ Mentor Teacher Initials ___________________

The Student Teaching Notebook: Keeping It All Together

The notebook is a vehicle through which the student teacher will be able to document professional growth. It is also a means of managing and organizing the overwhelming information that must be dealt with day-to-day, week-to-week, and month-to-month. In addition, the notebook provides the university supervisor with invaluable insight and important information regarding the student teacher's progress.

Notebook Organization

Student teachers are required to keep a notebook that contains and organizes all the information necessary to successfully complete the student teaching apprenticeship. A three-ring, 3-inch binder is strongly recommended, as information will be added to the notebook throughout the student teaching experience. The university supervisor evaluates the updated notebook, time card, and weekly reflection entries during each visit.

Notebook Sections

It is important to organize the notebook in a clear and thoughtful manner. The following sections should be included in the notebook. Since university supervisors must be able to locate specific information in the notebook quickly, they may prescribe a specific method of organization.

A. **Lesson Plans** — A lesson plan is a blueprint for instruction and classroom management. For examples of lesson plan formats, see pages 75-84 in this text. Be sure to note the subject/theme, time frame and date of each lesson. It is essential for student teachers to evaluate their lesson (initially) and their whole teaching day (during phases II and III). This activity facilitates growth and causes the student teacher to become a reflective practitioner.

B. **Weekly Progress Forms** — The mentor's weekly assessment, written observations, and specific suggestions should all be kept in this section. All written comments or suggestions offered by the mentor teacher about lesson plans and lesson delivery should be included as well. These forms may be found in the companion text, *Coaching the Special Education Student Teacher (Dual Certification)*.

C. **Weekly Reflection Entry** — Each week the student teacher will describe an event which occurred in the classroom, provide details about the event, describe their feelings and actions during the event, and what was learned from the event. (Note: Only the university supervisor will read the weekly reflection entries.)

D. **Timekeeping** — Since the timecard is a legal document, it should be kept in a page protector. The weekly time sheets are also kept in this section of the notebook.

E. **Calendar** — Keeping track of immediate and long-range deadlines is essential. Student teachers will need to integrate the information on the student teaching events calendar and the school's yearly calendar. The school's weekly updates are also helpful. In addition, this section of the notebook should include the Developmental Planning Chart, and the student teaching events calendar.

F. **Videotaping** — Student teachers are required to use videotaping to document their progress, identify areas that need improvement, and provide a sustained teaching opportunity for reflection.

It is quite common for a student teacher to feel self-conscious in front of a classroom full of students. To help the student teacher improve delivery skills, experienced mentors and university supervisors recommend using a video camera to tape the student teacher's performance. Student teachers privately watch the videotape using the "What Is Your Enthusiasm Rating?" chart (page 88) as a guide, focus on one feature at a time, and begin to analyze their performance.

G. **General Information** — In addition, the student teaching notebook may include a number of special features, such as:

* Class roster	* Attendance information
* Substitute plans	* District information and policies
* Grades	* Classroom management and
* Birthday chart	organization plan
* Phone numbers	* Class communications
* Duty schedule	- Parent Newsletter
* Transportation assignments	- Phone logs

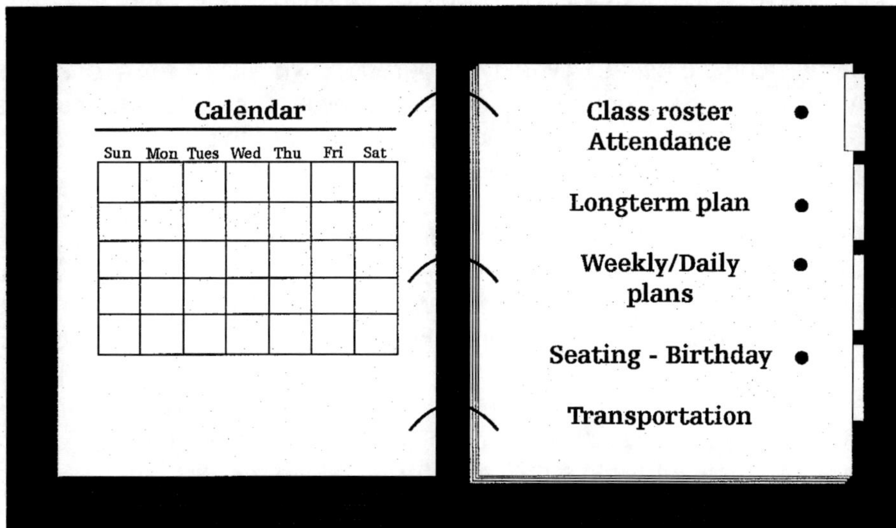

Chapter 4

Assessment: Instruments and Pedagogy

The purpose of assessment is to improve instruction by providing constructive feedback and to provide documentation of progress to the university. The assessment process is best served when the evaluator has frequent and regular opportunities to observe and provide feedback. Obviously, the mentor teacher serves as the main evaluator of the student teacher's daily performance in the classroom. Information about how the mentor facilitates the student teacher's ability to analyze his/her own instructional performance can be found in the companion text, *Coaching the Special Education Student Teacher (Dual Certification)*. While the mentor teacher has the main responsibility for observing the student teacher and providing feedback, the university supervisor plays a significant role in offering feedback to the student teacher as well.

Both the mentor/cooperating teacher's and university supervisor's observations are guided by two instruments; *The Professional Attributes and Characteristics Scale* and *The Instructional Development Scale*. Chapter 4 describes, in detail, the content of these two instruments in depth.

The following information provides a timeline of the weekly formative assessments, the more formal summative assessment, and the final evaluation. The following provides the time line for both options.

Regardless of whether the student teaching experience is 8 weeks, frequent feed-back is the key to improving the student teacher's skill. In addition to daily feedback, the mentor teacher completes the Weekly Progress Form. This form offers mentors an opportunity to review and document their perceptions, concerns, and suggestions. The Weekly Progress Forms are found in the forms section of this text. The student teacher is expected to keep all Weekly Progress Forms in their notebook.

Likewise the student teacher will need to be formally evaluated (fourth week for the 8-week experience). The formal evaluation documents the student teacher's progress and is reviewed with both the student teacher and the university supervisor. A copy of this form is sent to the Office of Professional Field Experience by the university supervisor.

During the final week, the mentor will complete the Final Evaluation which summarizes and reviews the student teacher's progress throughout the full-time apprenticeship. Information about the final evaluation is located in this text.

Professional Attributes and Characteristics Scale

The purpose of the Professional Attributes and Characteristics Scale is to provide the student teacher and the Office of Professional Field Experiences with specific information regarding the student teacher's character and disposition.

The indicators identified in the Professional Attributes and Characteristics Scale focus on qualities that successful teachers and good colleagues possess. Teaching also has an ethical dimension that requires a teacher to consistently consider the needs of the students (and the students' families), colleagues, administration, and the community at large. Successful teachers are individuals who demonstrate positive characteristics, such as integrity, perseverance and commitment. These traits are considered essential to success in the teaching profession. In essence, these attributes are the foundation to building a long-term career in education.

One copy of the Professional Attributes and Characteristics Scale is located in the Forms section of this handbook. Likewise, the Professional Attributes and Characteristics Scale is a part of the Weekly Progress Form. All of these forms can be found in *Coaching the Special Education Student Teacher (Dual Certification)*.

1. Attendance

Mentor teachers expect student teachers to be dedicated to the teaching profession. Daily attendance demonstrates a commitment to a successful student teaching experience. Student teachers demonstrate responsibility and dependability by daily participation and by appropriately notifying the mentor teacher and university supervisor if illness prevents them from attending.

1) Attendance

- ❑ Frequently absent
- ❑ Rarely absent
- ❑ Exemplary attendance

2. Punctuality

Schools function by the clock. Effective teachers value timelines and are responsive to the time-efficient demands of teaching. Student teachers should arrive at or before the designated starting time for teachers on their assigned campuses and consistently observe the mentor teacher's schedule. It is also extremely important to be punctual for duties, special classes, lunch, library, and special events.

2) Punctuality

- ❑ Frequently late
- ❑ Generally punctual
- ❑ Always on time

3. Professional Appearance

Teachers are role models for all students and are always in the public eye. Teachers need to dress in a professional manner. Likewise, student teachers need to ensure their general appearance is appropriate and consistent with district standards for professional dress.

---

3) Professional Appearance

- ❑ Occasionally appears inappropriately, unprofessionally dressed
- ❑ Is usually dressed appropriately
- ❑ Always dresses/appears professionally

---

4. Oral Expression

Effective teachers are articulate and communicate in a concise manner. Teachers must model grammatically correct language and fluent oral expression so children have consistent opportunities to hear appropriate language and imitate it. In addition, the "art" of teaching is greatly facilitated when the teacher is expressive and animated.

---

4) Oral Expression

- ❑ Makes frequent usage and/or grammatical errors
- ❑ Inarticulate
- ❑ Articulate
- ❑ Expressive, animated

---

5.   Written Expression

The teaching profession generates abundant opportunities for teachers to communicate effectively in writing. Newsletters, updates to parents and colleagues on the children's progress, referrals for special services, and Web pages/email are but a few examples of the need for clear, organized, and carefully crafted written expression.

---

5) Written Expression

- ❑ Written work contains misspellings and/or grammatical errors
- ❑ Written work is often unclear and disorganized
- ❑ Written work is organized and clearly expresses ideas
- ❑ Written work effectively communicates with parents, administrators, and/or colleagues

---

6.   Tact/Judgment

Teaching is a decision-making process. Social decisions are as important as appropriate instructional decisions; effective teachers demonstrate diplomacy and professional courtesy when handling difficult situations that may arise with parents, students, and colleagues. Listening and responding sensitively to others' views, as well as understanding what to do and say, demonstrate a teacher is confident and capable of making informed decisions that are in the best interest of students.

---

6) Tact/Judgment

- ❑ Thoughtless: highly insensitive to others' feelings and opinions
- ❑ Somewhat or sometimes insensitive and undiplomatic
- ❑ Perceptive: knows what to do or say in order to maintain good relations with others and responds accordingly
- ❑ Diplomatic: highly sensitive to others' feelings and opinions

---

7.   **Reliability/Dependability**

Teachers assume responsibility for the children's academic, emotional, and physical well-being. Effective teachers strive to anticipate the needs of both students and colleagues, and respond appropriately. Completing assigned tasks, gathering all necessary instructional materials prior to a lesson, attending school and district meetings on time, grading students' daily work, and preparing lesson plans are examples of behaviors that convey reliability and dependability.

---

7) Reliability/Dependability

- ❏ Sometimes fails to complete assigned tasks and duties
- ❏ Sometimes needs to be reminded to attend to assigned tasks/duties
- ❏ Responsible: attends to assigned tasks/duties on schedule without prompting
- ❏ Self-starter: perceives needs and attends to them immediately.

---

8.   **Self-Initiative/Independence**

Effective teachers are active and creative problem-solvers. They consistently analyze lessons, classroom interactions, and students' learning, and strive to find new ways to make learning efficient and exciting.

---

8) Self-Initiative/Independence

- ❏ Passive: depends on others for directions, ideas, and guidance
- ❏ Has good ideas, works effectively with limited supervision
- ❏ Creative and resourceful: independently implements plans

---

9. **Self-Confidence**

Teaching is a profession that requires one to be an independent problem-solver and an instantaneous decision-maker. Teachers must also be willing to take instructional risks. Likewise, teachers need to gain the confidence of students, colleagues, administrators, and parents. Hence, teachers must project a confidence in their abilities without appearing arrogant or conceited.

9) Self-Confidence

❑ Anxious: often appears self-conscious, nervous

❑ Arrogant: has unfounded belief in abilities

❑ Usually confident: comfortable in classroom situations

❑ Realistically self-assured: competently handles class demands

10. **Collegiality**

Effective teachers take advantage of working with and learning from other professionals. Developing warm, collegial, and supportive relationships with mentor teacher and colleagues also reduces professional isolation. Complimenting peers, sharing ideas and materials, listening to others' views, offering to help colleagues, or occasionally assuming a teammate's duty are ways of demonstrating a desire to become a part of the professional team.

10) Collegiality

❑ Often works in isolation

❑ Reluctant to share ideas and materials

❑ Often participates in team efforts

❑ Willingly shares ideas and materials

11.   Interaction With Students

Effective teachers establish a positive rapport with children that will assist them with classroom management and student discipline throughout the semester. Teachers must also demonstrate that they respect their students and are sensitive to their students' diverse academic, cultural, and personal needs. This is best accomplished by consistently monitoring children during learning, being accessible to students if they need additional help, being fair and consistent in applying rules and consequences, and demonstrating a warm, caring demeanor when interacting with students.

---

11) Interaction With Students

- ❑ Can appear threatening or antagonistic towards students
- ❑ Hesitant to work with students
- ❑ Relates easily and positively with students
- ❑ Outgoing: actively seeks opportunities to work with students

---

12.   Response to Students' Needs

Students in today's public school classroom have had vastly disparate experiences. Student teachers must be sensitive to students' socioeconomic, linguistic, cultural, and ethnic backgrounds, as well as learning styles and developmental differences. Student teachers can assist all children with their learning by varying instructional strategies and activities, providing immediate feedback to students, accepting individual learning styles, and praising children's' efforts as well as learning outcomes.

---

12) Response to Students' Needs

- ❑ Does not attempt to accommodate needs of unique learners
- ❑ Makes negative comments about students' ability to learn
- ❑ Usually accepts responsibility for all students' learning needs
- ❑ Consistently responds to learning needs of all students

---

13.   Response to Feedback

Teachers who wish to continue to grow professionally frequently seek advice on how to improve their teaching strategies. Effective teachers are open to suggestions and consistently consider how the suggestion might improve performance. In addition, effective teachers implement the suggestion, reflect on the benefits of the new technique, and practice it again so that the newly acquired strategy can become a part of the teaching repertoire.

---

13) Response to Feedback

❑ Defensive: unreceptive to feedback

❑ Receptive: but doesn't implement suggestions

❑ Receptive: and adjusts performance accordingly

❑ Eager: solicits suggestion and feedback from others

---

14.   Ability to Reflect and Improve Performance

Teaching is a dynamic process. Successful teachers consistently demonstrate a spirit of inquiry and curiosity. Effective teachers are self-analytical. They review many instructional options and consider how each idea would impact student learning and challenge classroom management. To develop as a teacher, student teachers should question mentor teachers' rationale for instructional decisions and actions, seek suggestions for improvement, and take time to review and assess each lesson.

---

14) Ability to Reflect and Improve Performance

❑ Reluctant to analyze teaching performance

❑ Makes some effort to review teaching skills

❑ Actively seeks ways to assess teaching abilities

❑ Consistently deepens knowledge of classroom practice and students' learning

---

15.   Professional Characteristics

<table>
<tr><td>Seldom Usually Always</td><td>For each characteristic, check the frequency indicator that is most reflective of the student teacher's behavior.</td></tr>
<tr><td>❏ ❏ ❏</td><td>Commitment: demonstrates genuine concern for students and is dedicated to the teaching profession</td></tr>
<tr><td>❏ ❏ ❏</td><td>Creativity: seeks opportunities to provide many unique learning experiences and develops imaginative lessons</td></tr>
<tr><td>❏ ❏ ❏</td><td>Flexibility: responds to unforeseen circumstances in appropriate manner and modifies actions or plans when necessary</td></tr>
<tr><td>❏ ❏ ❏</td><td>Integrity: maintains high ethical and professional standards and responds to district policies appropriately</td></tr>
<tr><td>❏ ❏ ❏</td><td>Organization: is efficient, successfully manages multiple tasks simultaneously, and maintains effective classroom routines/procedures</td></tr>
<tr><td>❏ ❏ ❏</td><td>Perseverance: strives to complete tasks and improve teaching skills, management strategies</td></tr>
<tr><td>❏ ❏ ❏</td><td>Positive disposition: possesses pleasant interpersonal skills, is patient, resilient, optimistic and approachable</td></tr>
</table>

16.   Potential as a Teacher

Teaching is a rewarding but demanding profession. The student teaching semester is the capstone field experience. Throughout the course of the semester the student teachers must demonstrate attributes and characteristics that indicate their commitment to the profession and their potential to teach. The mentor teacher will summarize the student teacher's professional attributes and characteristics by indicating a recommendation regarding the student's future in the profession.

16) Potential as a Teacher

❏ Recommend review of career options and consideration of profession other than teaching

❏ Recommend continuation in teaching profession

❏ Highly recommend continuation in teaching profession, strong candidate

Instructional Development Scale[*]

The purpose of the Instructional Development Scale (IDS) is to provide the student teacher and the Office of Professional Field Experiences with specific information regarding the student teacher's progress in developing consistent, competent instructional skills and teaching strategies. A sample of the trimester progress report is located in the Forms section of this text. The first and second trimester Instructional Development Scales are located in the Forms section of the companion text, *Coaching the Special Education Student Teacher (Dual Certification)*. The IDS consists of 26 items in three subsections:

> ➢ Designs and Plans Instruction
> ➢ Creates and Maintains a Learning Climate
> ➢ Implements and Manages Instruction and Assessment

The Instructional Development Scale is also prescriptive – it is designed to help the student teacher and mentor closely examine the complex activities of teaching. Each competency has been described and in many cases examples of specific teaching action have been provided.

---

[*] **Genealogy of the Instructional Development Scale**

The Instructional Development Scale (Enz, Freeman, Cook, Stamm & Kimerer, 1991) evolved from the Arizona Teacher Residency Instrument, ATRI (Warner, Hartgraves, Ryan, Reno & Brunstein, 1983) initially piloted at Northern Arizona University (Petersen, Maddux, Hatcher, Bernal & Williams, 1987) and Grand Canyon University (Horn 1989). The ATRI was further refined at Arizona State University and the Center for Educational Development in Tucson (Enz, Anderson, Weber, & Lawhead, 1992). All work on the ATRI was funded through the Arizona Department of Education through the Arizona Teacher Residency Program.

The Arizona Teacher Residency Instrument was based on the "Teacher Performance Assessment Instrument" at the University of Georgia in Athens (Capie, Anderson, Johnson & Ellett, 1979). The knowledge base for that instrument comes from The Beginning Teacher Evaluation Study (Fisher, Filby, Marliave, Cahen, Dishaw & Berliner, 1978), the Effective Teachers/Schools Research (Barr, 1929; Stallings & Kasbowckz, 1974; Doyle, 1978) and the Direct Model of Instruction (Rosenshine & Meyer, 1978)

The Latest edition of the Instructional Development Scale has been slightly refined to align with state and national teacher performance standards. (Enz, Carlile, Freeman, Cook, Stamm, and Kimerer, 1998).

Directions

a)   For each item, please mark only the descriptors (a, b, c and/or d) that were actually observed.

b)   Next, choose a level of overall proficiency (1, 2, 3, 4, or 5) for each item.

Level 1   Student teacher has not yet developed or used this skill.
Level 2   Student teacher is beginning to incorporate this skill.
Level 3   Student teacher uses this skill appropriately.
Level 4   Student teacher uses this skill appropriately and consistently.
Level 5   Student teacher uses this skill appropriately and consistently, with a high degree of competence and confidence.

NOTE: Proficiency level does not necessarily correspond to the number of descriptors that were checked.

---

12.   Manages Disruptive Behavior

①   ②   ③   ❹   ⑤

☑   a) Individuals who have caused disruptions are dealt with rather than the entire class being punished.
☑   b) Major disruptions are attended to quickly and appropriately.
☑   c) Consequences for misbehavior are based on the severity of the disruption.
☑   d) Disruptive behavior rarely occurs.

This section of the handbook provides specific information about each item and in some cases provides coaching hints to help the student teacher improve competency on this item.

NOTE: The Weekly Progress Form also includes a modified version of the Instructional Development Scale. This form has been designed to help the mentor give the student teacher written feedback on a weekly basis. These forms are located in the Forms section of the companion text, *Coaching the Special Education Student Teacher (Dual Certification)*.

Designs and Plans Instruction[*]

All teachers must be aware of district and state standards. Likewise, effective teachers know about their students' learning needs and interests. Both curriculum standards and students' needs must be considered when developing lesson plans. These standards must also be reflected in unit and daily lesson plans. As the apprenticeship progresses, the student teacher will need to develop all lesson plans, materials and resources necessary to deliver instruction. To make sure that important standards are being met, it is important to receive daily feedback from the mentor teacher.

All student teachers are required to write lesson plans for each lesson taught. Initially, all lesson plans should be quite detailed. As student teachers become more skilled at writing comprehensive plans, delivering lessons and managing students, their lesson plans can become more abbreviated. The form and format of the lesson plan must be agreed upon by the mentor teacher, university supervisor, and student teacher. Lesson plans will be submitted to the mentor teacher at least a day in advance of the lesson presentation.

Research support for this chapter includes: Berliner, 1982; Clark and Yinger, 1987 Hunter, 1982; Kronowitz, 1996; Shavelson, 1983 and 1987; Salomon, 1992; Schon, 1983; Shavelson and Borko, 1979.

1.   Specifies Desired Learner Outcomes for Lessons

Writing lesson plans is like planning a journey. If you expect to get where you want to go, you need to map your route carefully in order to make the most efficient use of time and resources. Likewise, teachers need to plan carefully to help children learn what is being taught and how to make full use of opportunities to connect curriculum content and involve students in the learning process.

<table>
<tr><td colspan="5">1. Specifies Desired Learner Outcomes for Lessons</td></tr>
<tr><td>①</td><td>②</td><td>③</td><td>④</td><td>⑤</td></tr>
</table>

❑   a) Desired learner outcome(s) described in clear and consistent terms

❑   b) Logically sequenced

❑   c) Appropriate to student achievement level(s)

❑   d) Directly linked to unit goals and to state, district, and school standards

a)   Desired learner outcome(s) described in clear and consistent terms

When the learning outcome contains a verb such as recall, solve, measure, or construct, the teacher will be able to determine the children's comprehension and level of involvement at given points in the lesson.

Example:

The student will be able to <u>label</u> the parts of a plan. "

b)   Logically sequenced

When children are asked to complete tasks in an order that is logical and builds naturally from one step to another, the teacher will spend more time teaching and less time keeping students on-task.

c)   Appropriate to student achievement level(s)

Children are more likely to stay with a task and subsequently learn more of the material taught *if* the material presented is already part of their prior experience. In addition, children must be presented materials with which they will experience a high rate of success. Students in fourth grade and higher should experience a success/accuracy rate of at least 80%. However, children in prekindergarten through third grade should experience a success rate of at least 90%.

**A high success rate is necessary for student
learning and achievement.**

d)   Directly linked to unit goals and to state/district/school standards

Children will learn best when the information builds upon and reinforces knowledge presented on previous days/weeks. This does not mean that learning always develops in a "lock-step," linear progression. Integrated instruction brings ideas together and forms connections in the learners' minds. Teachers who integrate curricula and relate the information to be learned to their students' lives increase the likelihood that the new information will be meaningful, relevant, and retained.

***Effective learning begins when the teacher knows
in what direction the lesson needs to go.***

		COGNITIVE PROCESS					
		KNOWLEDGE	COMPREHENSION	APPLICATION	ANALYSIS	SYNTHESIS	EVALUATION
EVOLUTION OF INSTRUCTION	INTRODUCTION	Count Recall Define Recite Draw Recognize Identify Record Indicate Repeat List State Name Tabulate Point Trace Quote Write Read	Associate Interpret Compare Interpolate Compute Predict Contrast Translate Describe Differentiate Discuss Distinguish Estimate Extrapolate				
	ELABORATION		Classify Compare Contrast	Apply Illustrate Calculate Practice Classify Relate Compete Solve Use Employ Examine Demonstrate	Utilize Order Group\ Transform		
	EXTENSION				Analyze Detect Explain Infer Separate Summarize Construct	Arrange Integrate Combine Organize Construct Plan Create Prepare Design Prescribe Develop Produce Formulate Propose Generalize Specify	Apprise Rank Assess Rate Critique Recommend Determine Select Evaluate Test Grade Judge Measure

(Adapted from Bloom, Engelhart, Frust, Hill, and Karthwohl, 1956)

Having clearly articulated learning outcomes also helps the teacher to determine the most appropriate type of student assessment. There are multiple types of measurements that assess students understanding. The following figure presents Bloom's Taxonomy with a list of outcomes that a teacher might choose as assessment measures.

Characteristics and Outcomes of Bloom's Taxonomy		
Level	**Characteristics**	**Outcomes**
Knowledge	Can recognize and recall specific terms, facts and symbols	• Label a picture • Generate a list • Complete a quiz
Comprehension	Can understand the main idea of material heard, viewed, or read	• Write brief report • Oral retelling of story
Application	Applies an abstract idea in a concrete situation, solves a problem or relates it to prior experiences	• Produce illustration or diagram/map/model • Solve problems • Teach others
Analysis	Examines a concept and determines its major components, sees the connections – cause-effects, similarities-differences.	• Graph, survey, chart, • Discuss cause-effect
Synthesis	Able to put together ideas in new and original ways.	• Artwork — song, poem, dance, music, plays, speech, video, film • Inventions — art work, blocks, dramatic play
Evaluation	Makes informed judgments about the value of ideas or materials	• Discussion • Expressing opinions • Ranking-comparisons

Planning the lesson includes planning the assessment.

2.   Specifies Teaching Procedures for Lessons

Knowing what needs to be taught/learned is only the first step in lesson planning. Just as critical is determining *how* to effectively deliver instruction. For beginning teachers, this may be a time-consuming process *but* the time spent mentally rehearsing, then writing the procedures, will help the student teacher be more successful in the actual delivery of the lesson.

The following indicators provide suggestions for achieving this competency.

---

2.   Specifies Teaching Procedures for Lessons

①   ②   ③   ④   ⑤

- ❑   a) Referenced to the objective(s)/outcomes
- ❑   b) Appropriate to accomplishing objective(s)/outcomes
- ❑   c) Logically sequenced
- ❑   d) Transitions are planned from one activity to another

---

a)   Referenced to the objective(s)/outcomes

This refers to the written organization of the actual lesson plan. Which procedures will accomplish what objective?

Objective/Outcome	Procedures	Resources	Assessment
#1.	1(a) 1(b) 1(c)	1(a) 2(b) 3(c)	#1.
#2.	2(a) 2(b) 2(c)	2(a) 2(b) 2(c)	#2.

b) **Appropriate to accomplishing objective(s)/outcomes**

When the teacher does not take time to think about how he/she will teach the content, the result often means that procedures are not appropriate to accomplish the desired learner outcome.

Example (Correct Procedure):

<u>Outcome:</u>   Students will define the term "solar system."

<u>Procedures:</u>   Students practice telling definition to neighbor.
This activity <u>will</u> accomplish the goal!

Example (Incorrect Procedure):

<u>Outcome:</u>   Students will define the term "solar system."

<u>Procedures:</u>   Students copy names of planets.
Students label planets on map of solar system.
(Labeling planets will not help students learn to define solar system.)
Though the students will be busy, this activity <u>will not</u> accomplish the stated learning outcome.

c) **Logically sequenced**

Part of effective teaching involves knowing what to do and in what order to do it. The first part of the lesson should establish the foundation; the next information task expands children's knowledge by building on this foundation.

d) **Transitions are planned from one activity to another**

Efficient transitions from one learning activity to another save valuable class time and prevent disruptive student behavior. Smooth transitions don't usually occur naturally; they must be planned.

3.   **Specifies Resources for Lessons**

Some teachers lock themselves into using only the basic textbook or workbook. Basic texts and workbooks will give students just that — the basics. Effective primary teachers go beyond basic materials and offer students an opportunity to learn from a variety of resources. When teachers draw from a variety of resources, they are more likely to provide students with multiple ways to learn the material being taught.

Consider the following descriptors when identifying resources:

<table>
<tr><td colspan="6">3.   Specifies Resources for Lessons</td></tr>
<tr><td></td><td>①</td><td>②</td><td>③</td><td>④</td><td>⑤</td></tr>
<tr><td>❑</td><td colspan="5">a) Relevance to learning activity</td></tr>
<tr><td>❑</td><td colspan="5">b) Lesson plans include specific description of resources, such as title, page, and equipment</td></tr>
<tr><td>❑</td><td colspan="5">c) Concrete or manipulative materials identified when appropriate</td></tr>
<tr><td>❑</td><td colspan="5">d) Creative use of resources</td></tr>
</table>

a)   **Relevance to learning activity**

Resources are appropriate and facilitate learning rather than distract from it, or, "Is it necessary to bring in an elephant to teach the color 'gray'?"

b)   **Lesson plans include specific description of resources, such as title, page, and equipment**

Always remember that tomorrow you might be absent. Could a substitute teacher present the lesson you were planning to teach?

c)   **Concrete or manipulative materials identified when appropriate**

When beginning teachers plan activities, it is important to list all of the materials necessary to accomplish the task. The very act of writing the list helps teachers to mentally rehearse the delivery of the lesson.

d)   Creative use of resources

Imaginative use of materials will make learning fun for the children and exciting for the student teacher. Resources can also include:

- ➢ Speakers, experts on particular subjects
- ➢ CD-ROMS, videotapes, audiotapes, compact discs, digital cameras, and other multimedia devices
- ➢ Computers with Internet connection
- ➢ Art supplies
- ➢ Cooking/sewing supplies
- ➢ P.E. equipment
- ➢ Musical instruments
- ➢ Math manipulatives
- ➢ Puppets
- ➢ Maps
- ➢ Trade books

Creative resources enhance learning opportunities.

4.   **Specifies Procedures for Assessing Student Progress**

4.   Specifies Procedures for Assessing Student Progress

①   ②   ③   ④   ⑤

❑   a) Written lesson plans include informal assessment of student learning

❑   b) Tests and other formal assessments focus directly on instructional goals and objectives, and assesses only the content that was taught

❑   c) Develops and maintains an accurate record of student performance

❑   d) Considers multiple sources of assessment data when making instructional decisions

a)   Written lesson plans include informal assessments of student learning

When should the teacher assess student progress?

Children's' understanding should be assessed at significant points throughout the entire lesson. This includes constant monitoring of children's performance or occasionally pausing the lesson to ask or observe if all learners can demonstrate their understanding of the information being taught.

How can the teacher determine if all students can perform correctly?

Beyond observation, the teacher may ask children to write the answer, tell a neighbor, respond in unison, indicate the answer on individual slates, signal the answer, demonstrate the skill, etc.

Why should teachers assess students frequently?

Before the teacher proceeds from one goal to the next, all children need to demonstrate an understanding of the content presented. If all students do not understand the lesson, the teacher will need to adjust teaching strategies, try again, and then reassess the students' progress to determine understanding before moving on to the next objective.

b) Tests and other formal assessments focus directly on instructional goals and objectives, and assess only the content that was taught

No surprises — test *how* and *what* you taught. Objectives assessed in end-of-unit tests must be consistent with information presented during daily lessons. This means that when the teacher gives a test or exam, questions should be taken directly from daily lesson objectives and the teacher should have already observed each child's correct daily performance.

c) Develops and maintains an accurate record of student performance

Teachers need to develop and maintain a management system for accurately collecting and recording data of student progress.

d) Considers multiple sources of assessment data when making important decisions

Based on daily observations and ongoing documentation, the student teacher should be familiar with the students' strengths and limitations. Official tests only supplement what the teacher already knows. Student teachers should also establish the habit of making anecdotal notes that describe their students' interactions and activities. This can be accomplished by carrying note cards or a note pad to date and record observations and patterns of behavior for each student.

Teachers of younger students should maintain portfolios of children's work. Older students should be taught how to maintain their own work folders and actively engage in self-assessment and documentation of their achievement.

The following page reviews a number of approaches that special education teachers might use to collect information about children's progress.

Assessment Checklist

Directions: Observe your mentor teacher to determine what approaches he or she typically uses to collect information about children's development and their progress. Place a check by the tools/techniques used; write any comments, suggestions, or additions he/she describes; then summarize what you learned about assessment from this interview.

I. Teacher Observations —The most sensitive student assessment is teacher observation. In all cases, the teacher labels, dates, and organizes the observation records to document development over time.

- ☐ Checklists: Sometimes called structured observation. The teacher uses predetermined observation guides to document students' development and progress on specific skills or concepts.
- ☐ Anecdotal records: Sometimes called unstructured observation. The teacher records student interactions with peers, print, literature, writing process, in-class discussion, center activities, etc.
- ☐ Vignettes. Sometimes called teacher reflections. The teacher recalls student interactions and records them after the event has occurred.

II. Interviews/Questions Techniques — Interviews may be conducted with the student, parents, and special area teachers. Interviews may occur informally during the school day or may be formalized when the teacher needs to narrow the focus of the questions to reflect a previously identified concern.   Teachers may consider four types of interview questions:

- ☐ Descriptive: What did you do during___________?
- ☐ Structured: Can you tell me when __________?
- ☐ Contrast: How are these stories alike/different?
- ☐ Process: How did you decide to _____________?

III. Student Self-Assessment Techniques — Students should be actively involved in assessing their own work, reflecting upon their progress, and establishing new learning goals.

- ☐ Teacher-made questionnaires/surveys.
- ☐ Teacher-student conferences.

IV. Products, Work Samples and Artifacts — Teacher collects multiple examples of child created products to assess each student's development. Some products, such as samples of students' writing, can be gathered together in a folder. If the students' original works cannot be saved (e.g., an art project), a photograph can be made of the product. Because memories are short, the teacher or the student should record a brief description of the product or the activity that resulted in the product. For example:

- ☐ Journal entries
- ☐ Learning logs
- ☐ Formal written assignments
- ☐ Portfolios
- ☐ Student presentations

. **V Portfolio Management System** - Teacher devises a management system to collect and analyze samples of students' work, teacher's anecdotal notes, and formal and informal assessment measures. A portfolio allows the teacher to document a student's progress over time and share that information with the student, the student's parents, and other teachers and administrators.

Many teachers find that folders with pockets and center clasps for three-hole-punched paper serve as better storage containers than file folders. Interview forms, running-record sheets, and other assessments can be three-hole-punched, thus permitting their easy insertion into each student's folder. When anecdotal notes and vignettes are written on computer mailing labels, the labels can be attached to the inside covers of each student's folder. When these notes are written on index cards, the cards can be stored in one of the folder's pockets. Also, a sandwich bag might be stapled inside each student's folder to hold an audiotape. The self-sealing feature of the bag means that the tape can be securely held inside the folder. The class folders might be housed in a plastic container or in hanging files in a file cabinet.

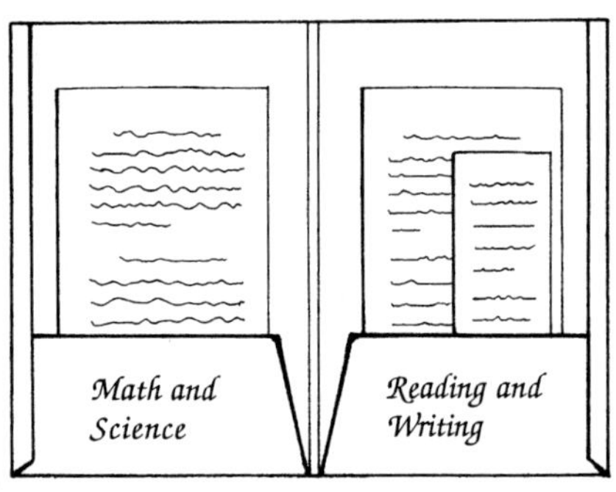

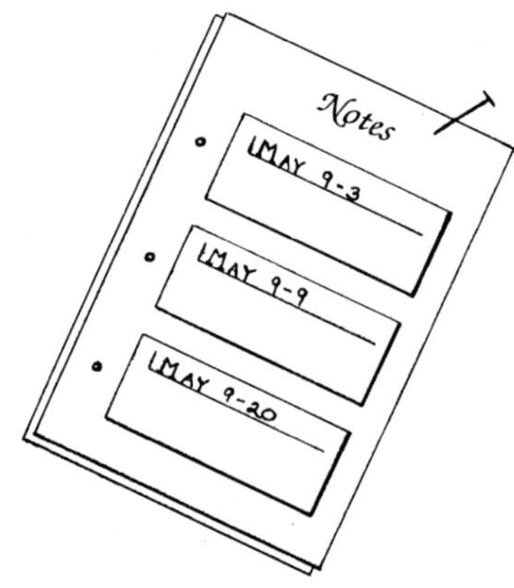

5. Plans for Student Diversity, Abilities and Styles

Not all children process information in the same way. If they did, teaching would be easy and learning guaranteed! As there is a continuum of instructional theories, there is a corresponding range of learning preferences. Being able to recognize and respond to students' unique learning needs is one of the greatest challenges in teaching.

<table>
<tr><td colspan="6">5.   Plans for Student Diversity, Abilities, and Styles</td></tr>
<tr><td></td><td>①</td><td>②</td><td>③</td><td>④</td><td>⑤</td></tr>
<tr><td>❑</td><td colspan="5">a) Presents instruction based on assessment of students' performance</td></tr>
<tr><td>❑</td><td colspan="5">b) Provides remedial or enrichment materials and instruction when appropriate</td></tr>
<tr><td>❑</td><td colspan="5">c) Plans student/parent conferences to discuss progress</td></tr>
<tr><td>❑</td><td colspan="5">d) Varies instructional strategies in accordance with student needs</td></tr>
</table>

a) Presents instruction based on assessment of students' performance

Even within a single grade level, students' abilities, learning styles, language and culture, knowledge base, and interests are extremely varied. Therefore, student teachers need to plan for these diverse student needs.

Current instruction should be based on the continuous assessment of children's performance. Assignments should be varied depending on each child's needs. Students' learning is greatly impaired if the material far exceeds or vastly underestimates their current knowledge and experience.

Keeping track of the students' levels and abilities may be a challenge to the student teacher. Keeping a grading/progress chart can be quite helpful.

	Achieved # Facts 1-10	Achieved # Facts 11-20	Achieved "+" Exchange or Trade
John	10/3/10	10/28/10	
Sally	10/7/10	10/28/10	
Jose	10/1/10	11/6/10	
Ra Val	11/6/10		

b) **Provides remedial or enrichment materials/instruction when appropriate**

Many assignments and projects are "self-adjusting." This means that all children will be able to do them to some degree, but more proficient students will simply be able to do more in less time. Sometimes children may be given a choice of projects to work on (ranging from very easy to quite complex) and, with teacher guidance, the students can select their own "level."

The challenge of providing instruction to children with varying abilities can also be dealt with by providing supplementary material, and resources for both ends of the continuum. Additional demonstration or explanation during guided practice times often helps students who are having difficulty.

c) **Plans student/parent conferences to discuss progress**

When children are provided with appropriate feedback, they will become more easily motivated and are more likely to experience success. Children should be encouraged to assess their own performance, and discuss and determine their own learning goals. Likewise, parents should be fully and consistently informed about their child's performance.

d) **Varies instructional strategies in accordance with student needs**

Variety is not only the spice of life, it is essential for teaching. Deciding when to teach directly and when to facilitate learning through personal discovery is part of the art of teaching.

6.   Plans Address All Levels of Knowledge and Understanding

<table>
<tr><td colspan="6">6.   Plans Address All Levels of Knowledge and Understanding</td></tr>
<tr><td></td><td>①</td><td>②</td><td>③</td><td>④</td><td>⑤</td></tr>
<tr><td>❑</td><td colspan="5">a) Plans require students to memorize important vs. trivial information and to comprehend or interpret information as appropriate</td></tr>
<tr><td>❑</td><td colspan="5">b) Plans require students to apply information to real life settings</td></tr>
<tr><td>❑</td><td colspan="5">c) Plans require students to identify/clarify complex ideas or to synthesize knowledge by integrating information</td></tr>
<tr><td>❑</td><td colspan="5">d) Plans stress depth as well as breadth of content coverage</td></tr>
</table>

a)   Plans require students to memorize important vs. trivial information and to comprehend or interpret information as appropriate

There are potentially thousands of facts and details in every content lesson but only a few serve as foundations for learning. The challenge student teacher's face is deciding which information is most relevant for children to learn and then structuring lessons and assessments reflecting that emphasis.

b)   Plans require students to apply information to real-life settings

Information should be learned for a purpose beyond passing the test. Material that can be applied in real life has a greater chance of being retained and understood.

c)   Plans require students to identify/clarify complex ideas or to synthesize knowledge by integrating information

Research by Benjamin Bloom (1956) indicates that more than 95% of all test items students encounter ask for little more than simple recall of information. Bloom has developed six categories of thinking. These categories provide a framework for designing activities to help extend and improve students' thinking. Examples of questions that correspond to the six categories of thinking can be found on page 76.

d)   Plans stress depth as well as breadth of content coverage

It must be remembered that children need to have information they can understand before they are asked to think at any of the higher levels. Often teachers are so eager to promote higher-level thinking that they do not make certain the students have adequate knowledge and understanding of basic concepts.

Higher-level thinking skills are difficult to teach to children who have not developed confidence in their own ability to learn because of experiencing failure and frustration at the foundational levels of thinking.

BLOOM'S TAXONOMY

Primary example: The Three Little Pigs	**Intermediate Example:** Pledge of Allegiance
KNOWLEDGE: This level of thinking involves the student recognizing or remembering something that was learned.	
What type of materials did the 3 little pigs use to build their houses?	Say the Pledge of Allegiance.
COMPREHENSION: This level requires comprehension or interpretation of information.	
Why didn't the third little pig's house blow down?	Say the Pledge of Allegiance in your own words.
APPLICATION: At the application level, the student is required to solve a problem or complete a task in a situation which is new.	
If the wolf came to your home, would he be able to blow it down?	What do liberty and justice on the playground mean?
ANALYSIS: The student breaks the information down and looks for relationships between parts.	
What part of the story could not have actually happened?	What elements do all pledges have?
SYNTHESIS: At this level, the student originates or combines ideas in order to create a totally new product or plan.	
How would this story be different if it were told from the wolf's point of view?	Write a class pledge.
EVALUATION: The student makes assessments and gives reasons to support a particular position.	
Do you think it was right for the pigs to boil the wolf at the end of the story? Why or why not?	Should everyone say the pledge? Support your position.

Planning for Instruction and Learning

What type of instructional strategy should I use?

Effective teachers use a variety of instructional strategies to ensure that all children's unique learning styles are accommodated. Depending on the particular lesson, teaching methods may include direct instruction, cooperative learning, inquiry, discussion, concept attainment, and concept generalization that involve students in a variety of ways.

Effective teachers also use strategies that engage students' minds in a variety of ways, ranging from recall of basic facts to application of knowledge in meaningful, creative endeavors. When teachers use strategies that include higher-level thinking activities, they provide valuable opportunities for students to do such things as compare and contrast ideas, solve problems, formulate hypotheses, and create new products.

Student teachers are encouraged to use a range of instructional strategies. Regardless of the strategy, student teachers are required to <u>write</u> plans for instruction. The following section presents two lesson formats — direct instruction and 5-E. Models of both are provided.

What lesson plan format should I use?

Teachers will eventually develop a lesson plan format that best suits their instructional and organizational style. However, at the beginning of the student teaching semester, student teachers are required to use one of the following formats — direct instruction format or inquiry learning lesson plan format. A lesson plan written early in the semester should be quite detailed. Student teachers are required to provide a copy of their lesson plan to the mentor teacher at least a day prior to instruction. This allows the mentor an opportunity to offer advice which usually improves lesson effectiveness and enhances student management. **Since the mentor teacher is legally responsible for curriculum and instruction, it is essential that the mentor initial each lesson plan after it is reviewed and approved.** The lesson formats presented on pages 75-83 are examples of lesson plans designed for art teachers.

> **NOTE:** Regardless of instructional approach or teaching strategy, all lessons should be anchored to district/state curriculum goals/standards.

What should I consider when I plan lessons?

As a student teacher develops lesson plans, it is important that the following key questions are answered.

State Standard:	District Goal:

<u>Learner Outcome</u>: What should the student know or do after this lesson?

- ➢ What is the purpose of this lesson?

- ➢ Why is this information important?

- ➢ What skills do these students possess?

- ➢ How can students be engaged/motivated to learn this concept?

- ➢ How can this information be expanded?

<u>Procedure:</u> What is the best way to involve the learners?

- ➢ How should the lesson be presented?

    - ◆ Direct instruction

    - ◆ Concept generalization

    - ◆ Inquiry

- ➢ Any adaptive instruction/learning accommodations?

- ➢ What resource materials would support this lesson?

- ➢ What monitoring and adjusting techniques could be used?

- ➢ How much time will be needed?

<u>Assessment</u>: What measures would best reflect students' learning?

- ➢ What formal or informal assessment measure should be used?

- ➢ Should an assignment be planned to reinforce learning?

- ➢ How should this lesson be closed?

DIRECT INSTRUCTION FORMAT

Subject:	**Class/Period:**
Date:	

LEARNER OUTCOMES: Lesson objective and subobjectives

State Standard   District Outcome

ANTICIPATORY SET: Focus, introduction, and motivation

INSTRUCTIONAL INPUT: Teaching procedures and student activities

ACCOMMODATIONS: Adjustments for students with specific learning needs

EVALUATION: Checking for understanding and lesson assessment

CLOSURE: Lesson summation of learner's new knowledge

ASSIGNMENTS: Independent practice and homework

RESOURCES: Equipment, materials, and teaching aids

Lesson Plan — Direct Instruction

Kindergarten State Standards — Workplace Skills Standards (Kindergarten)

Standard 1 — Students use principles of effective oral, written/listening communication skills to make decisions and solve workplace problems.

    1WP-R1. Follow simple directions and PO2. Complete directed work

Objective: Students will line up for recess in an orderly manner with 100% accuracy.

Anticipatory Set: Ask children to close their eyes and imagine what it would be like if everyone in class got up at the same time and tried to go out the front door. Today we are going to learn how to line up in a safe and orderly manner.

Input (teaching procedures)
- Explain safety issues (feet getting stepped on, people getting shoved)
- Explain procedures for lining up at the door
  - Wait for row to be called
  - Line up single file
  - Stand in line quietly

Check for Understanding: Ask children to think about the three steps and then whisper to a neighbor what they think they are. Then randomly call on students to name the procedures for lining up for recess and have the rest of the class give a thumbs-up if they agree with what is said and a thumbs-down if they don't.

Modeling: Model what it looks like to get out of the seat, line up single file in a row, and stand quietly.

Guided Practice: Have entire class practice lining up at the door a few times. Teacher will give active feedback during the process.

Independent Practice: The children will line up without teacher feedback in the correct order as presented in the lesson.

Closure: Ask children to close their eyes again and imagine what the class looks like when it lines up correctly. Call on children to review the three steps for lining up. Ask children to remember what they have learned in this lesson and to use it every time for the rest of the school year when they are asked to line up. Tell them that later today you are going to check to see if they remember this lesson when it is time to line up for recess.

Evaluation: Students will be evaluated on their skill at being able to line up in an orderly manner with 100% accuracy.

Accommodations/Modifications: For any student with a physical disability, they may need to be allowed extra time to get in line and may benefit from having a peer buddy provide assistance if necessary. Make sure the child has room to move freely around the classroom by widening rows between desks or areas of student traffic.

Five E Lesson Format

The Five E's (Engagement, Exploration, Explanation, Extension, and Evaluation) is designed for the inquiry nature of guiding and science lessons (Gagne, Briggs & Wager, 1992). It more closely aligns with a combination of the cognitive information processing and constructivist perspectives of learning.

Five E Science Lesson Plan

Engagement: The activities in this section capture the students' attention, stimulate their thinking, and help them access prior knowledge.	<ul><li>Demonstration<ul><li>teacher and/or student</li></ul></li><li>Reading from a<ul><li>current media release</li><li>science journal or book</li><li>piece of literature (biography, essay, poem, etc)</li></ul></li><li>Free write</li><li>Analyze a graphic organizer</li></ul>
Exploration: In this section students are given time to think, plan, investigate, and organize collected information.	<ul><li>Reading authentic resources to collect information<ul><li>to answer open-ended questions</li><li>to make a decision</li></ul></li><li>Solve a problem</li><li>Construct a model</li><li>Experiment design and/or perform</li></ul>
Explanation: Students are now involved in an analysis of their exploration. Their understanding is clarified and modified because of reflective activities.	<ul><li>Student analysis and explanation</li><li>Supporting ideas with evidence</li><li>Reading and discussion</li></ul>
Extension: This section gives students the opportunity to expand and solidify their understanding of the concept and/or apply it to a real-world situation.	<ul><li>Problem solving</li><li>Experimental inquiry</li><li>Thinking skills activities</li><li>Classifying, abstracting, error analysis</li><li>Decision-making</li></ul>
Evaluation: By the end of the lesson there should be a means of determining how well students have learned and can apply the new concepts and the related vocabulary. Such evaluation does not have to be at the end of the lesson. It can be embedded in other phases.	<ul><li>Teacher- and/or student-generated scoring tools or rubrics</li></ul>

5-E Lesson Plan Example

Lesson Title: Camouflage: Eating All the Little Fishes

Lesson Outcome: The first graders will learn how camouflage helps animals survive.

Engagement: Teacher reads the story "How to Hide a Butterfly and Other Insects" by Ruth Heller. This simple text has color pictures that demonstrate how insects use camouflage to hide from their enemies and prey. The first graders have fun looking for the hidden insects.

Exploration: The teacher breaks the children into six groups of four students each.

- Each group has a different-colored, patterned cloth that is placed on the table, and each table had a tiny cup containing many different-colored paper "fish."
- The "fish" are sprinkled on the cloth.
- The teacher turns out the lights.
- The children are asked to find as many of the fish as they can and remove them from the cloth.
- The children have 20 seconds to find all the fish they can.
- The teacher turns the light back on and the children freeze.
- The fish left are sorted and counted by color.

Explanation: The teacher asks the children if they notice anything about the fish that are left on the cloth. The children in each group should realize that the fish left are the same color as the cloth.

Extension: The teacher asks the children to think about, then write, their explanation of how the fish in their experiment are like the butterflies and insects in the story, "How to Hide a Butterfly and Other Insects." The teacher gives each group chart paper and markers to record their thoughts.

Evaluation: The teacher gives each child drawing paper and crayons. The teacher asks the children to draw a habitat (a concept previously learned) — and to draw pictures of camouflaged animals that might live in this habitat. As the children complete this task, the teacher circulates and asks children about their unique creations.

Accommodations/Modifications: A student who has difficulty with attention (i.e. ADD), or a student with a visual impairment, or mental retardation may need further structure throughout the lesson so as not to get distracted or "lost" in the inquiry-based approach. It may be necessary for the teacher or an aide to provide structure by restating instructions, scaffolding support, providing written directions in a checklist format to ensure students stay on task.

SELF-EVALUATION OF LESSON

Student teachers need to assess the quality of each lesson they teach. The following questions may guide the student teacher's reflection. Make copies of this page to use throughout the semester.

MOTIVATION: How effective was the introduction? Was there a meaningful connectiong to children? Was it sufficient to properly motivate the class or classes? If it was not effective, how could it have been improved?

LENGTH OF LESSON: Was the timeframe for the lesson adhered to? Was there adequate time for the material to be presented? Were transitions completed quickly? If the lesson was too long or too short, explain why.

LEARNER SUCCESS: Were the students engaged in the learning? Did all students have access to lesson concepts? Did the lesson use multiple learning strategies and activities? How was the lesson given to accommodate special needs learners?

LESSON COMMENTS: Generalize regarding the success of the lesson or the difficulties encountered. Consider voice, grammar, speech habits, students attention or inattention, level of content (too technical or too basic), etc. If the same lesson is given to two or more classes, keep comments general enough to include the sum total of your experiences.

SUGGESTIONS FOR IMPROVEMENT: As a result of the reflections on this lesson:
What are the strengths of this lesson?

What should be done next time to improve it?

Creates and Maintains a Learning Climate

Effective teachers develop positive learning environments and build classroom community. When students feel safe and accepted, they are more likely to be actively involved in the learning.

Research support for this chapter includes: Brandt, 1984; Bondy, Ross, Gallingane, & Hambacher, 2007;. Brophy, 1987; Brophy & Evertson, 1976; Evertson & Weinstein,.2006; Honig, Miller, & Church, 2006; Lasley, 1981; Moyles, 2006; Stipek, 1986.

7. Communicates Enthusiasm for Student Learning

What is *enthusiastic* teaching?

- ➢ Stimulating

- ➢ Animated

- ➢ Energetic

- ➢ Mobile

<table>
<tr><td colspan="6">7.   Communicates Enthusiasm for Student Learning</td></tr>
<tr><td></td><td>①</td><td>②</td><td>③</td><td>④</td><td>⑤</td></tr>
<tr><td>❑</td><td colspan="5">a) Eye contact or facial expressions communicate pleasure, concern, interest, etc.</td></tr>
<tr><td>❑</td><td colspan="5">b) Voice inflections stress points of interest and importance.</td></tr>
<tr><td>❑</td><td colspan="5">c) Communicates enthusiasm through movement in the classroom.</td></tr>
<tr><td>❑</td><td colspan="5">d) Gestures accentuate points.</td></tr>
</table>

a) Eye contact or facial expressions communicate pleasure, concern, interest, etc.

All things being equal, teachers who present material with appropriate gesture, animation, and eye contact will have students who achieve better on tests than will teachers who do not gesture, talk in a monotone, and generally behave in an unenthusiastic manner.

Eye contact is especially important in dealing with disruptive behaviors. When the teacher looks a student straight in the eye, it usually communicates, "I really mean it."

b) Voice inflections stress points of interest and importance

Most children respond more positively to variance in voice inflection than they do to monotone. Studies on the effects of voice inflection have shown that variety in pitch and intensity affects receptivity of the listener. Additionally, *where* the inflection is place affects credibility of the sender.
Examples:
*It's time to take out your math books? **Or** It's **time** to take out your math books.*

c) Communicates enthusiasm through movement in the classroom

Teachers who easily move about the whole classroom encourage on-task behavior and maintain higher levels of the children's attention than teachers who stay close to the chalkboard. In addition, movement through the class greatly reduces misbehavior.

d) Gestures accentuate points

Researchers report that of all the parts of the human body used to transmit information, the hands are the most powerful. Effective teachers are very aware of the importance of body language in teaching students and consistently use their whole body to communicate.

WHAT'S YOUR ENTHUSIASM RATING?

EXAMPLE: In the third week of student teaching, Sarah was frustrated with the second-grade children for becoming restless during whole-group, read-aloud time. Sarah's mentor suggested she videotape her lesson and demonstrated how to use the "What Is Your Enthusiasm Rating?" chart. That evening Sarah focused on each of the items listed on the chart, beginning with vocal delivery for 20 seconds. At the end of the 20-second observation, she placed a tally mark beside the descriptors that best described her vocal delivery performance. Next, she focused on the eyes feature for 20 seconds, then assessed. She repeated this 20-second observation rotation for the entire 25-minute lesson.

As Sarah reviewed her tally marks, she acknowledged that her gestures and body movements were, by necessity, rated "low" since she was reading a book sitting down. She felt her eyes and facial expressions were "medium." Since she was reading from a text, she put a NA (not applicable) for word selection. She also marked herself low on acceptance of ideas and feelings because she did not realize she had hurried when the children began to misbehave. However, she was surprised that her voice was not projecting and that she had difficulty hearing herself on the tape. She was sure that most of the children couldn't hear either!

The next day Sarah and her mentor discussed ways to help Sarah increase her volume. Sarah commented that she had never had any prior opportunity to learn to *feel and hear* the sound of her voice in real classroom conditions, which included speaking over the hum of the air conditioning and the distractions of the classes outside on the playground. Within a few days Sarah had learned how to *hear* herself and was also learning to ask predicting questions and acknowledge the children's comments. All of these improvements made story time a pleasure for both Sarah and her students.

Features		Low	Medium	High
VOCAL DELIVERY		卌 卌 1		
		monotone, limited inflection, poor articulation.	variations of pitch, volume and speed; good articulation.	great and sudden changes in volume, tone and pitch.
EYES			卌 卌 1	
		looks dull or bored: avoids eye contact; often maintains a blank stare.	appears interested; occasionally lighting up, shining.	dancing, opening wide, eyebrows raised; maintains eye contact.
GESTURES		卌 卌 1		
		keeps arms at sides or folded, appears rigid.	often points, occasional sweeping motion using body, head, arms, hands, and	quick and demonstrative, changes pace, energetic; natural body movements.
BODY MOVEMENTS		卌 卌 1		
		seldom moves from one spot or from sitting to standing position.	moves freely, slowly and steadily.	changes pace, unpredictable and energetic; natural body
FACIAL EXPRESSION			卌 卌 1	
		appears deadpan; expressionless.	agreeable; smiles frequently; looks pleased, happy or sad if situation calls for.	appears vibrant; shows many expressions.
WORD SELECTION		NA		
		mostly nouns, few descriptors or adjectives; simple or trite expressions.	some descriptors or adjectives or repetition of the same ones.	highly descriptive; uses many adjectives.
ACCEPTANCE OF IDEAS/FEELINGS		卌 卌 1		
		little indications of acceptance; may ignore students' feelings or ideas.	accepts ideas and feelings; praises or clarifies; some variations in response.	quick to accept, praise, encourage many variations in response.
OVERALL ENERGY LEVEL		卌 卌 1		
		lethargic; appears inactive, dull.	appears energetic and demonstrative.	exuberant; high degree of energy and vitality; highly

Table title: "What is Your Enthusiasm Rating?" - Example

Adopted from Gephart, Strothers and Duckett, 1981).

"What is Your Enthusiasm Rating?"			
Features	**Low**	**Medium**	**High**
VOCAL DELIVERY	monotone, limited inflection, poor articulation.	variations of pitch, volume and speed; good articulation.	great and sudden changes in volume, tone and pitch.
EYES	looks dull or bored: avoids eye contact; often maintains a blank stare.	appears interested; occasionally lighting up, shining.	dancing, opening wide, eyebrows raised; maintains eye contact.
GESTURES	keeps arms at sides or folded, appears rigid.	often points, occasional sweeping motion using body, head, arms, hands, and face.	quick and demonstrative, changes pace, energetic; natural body movements.
BODY MOVEMENTS	seldom moves from one spot or from sitting to standing position.	moves freely, slowly and steadily.	changes pace, unpredictable and energetic; natural body
FACIAL EXPRESSION	appears deadpan; expressionless.	agreeable; smiles frequently; looks pleased, happy or sad if situation calls for.	appears vibrant; shows many expressions.
WORD SELECTION	mostly nouns, few descriptors or adjectives; simple or trite expressions.	some descriptors or adjectives or repetition of the same ones.	highly descriptive; uses many adjectives.
ACCEPTANCE OF IDEAS/FEELINGS	little indications of acceptance; may ignore students' feelings or ideas.	accepts ideas and feelings; praises or clarifies; some variations in response.	quick to accept, praise, encourage many variations in response.
OVERALL ENERGY LEVEL	lethargic; appears inactive, dull.	appears energetic and demonstrative.	exuberant; high degree of energy and vitality; highly

Adopted from Gephart, Strothers and Duckett, 1981).

8. Demonstrates Warmth and Friendliness

<table>
<tr><td>8.</td><td colspan="5">Demonstrates Warmth and Friendliness</td></tr>
<tr><td></td><td>①</td><td>②</td><td>③</td><td>④</td><td>⑤</td></tr>
</table>

□   a) Asks about students' interests and opinions

□   b) Interacts in a relaxed and informal way with students

□   c) Moves freely among students

□   d) Uses students' names in a warm and friendly way

a) Asks about students' interests and opinions

"No one cares how much you know, until they know how much you care."

Children reap significant benefits as teachers get to know them. This knowledge actually improves students' learning and strengthens the classroom community. All children have some special interest that teachers can recognize, build on, and relate to. When a teacher shows interest in a child his/her self-esteem soars. In addition, research suggests that children learn best when engaged in activities they care about; hence, when teachers incorporate students' interest into daily activities, the learning process becomes relevant and exciting.

There are many ways teachers can learn about their students' interests. Ask the students open-ended questions about their favorite things to do after school, favorite book, favorite TV show, etc. Dialogue or interactive journals are another wonderful way to get to know your students. One exciting approach is to have lunch with a few children once a week. Finally, invite hard-to-know children to assist you with some project before or after school for a few minutes — it will be time well spent for both of you.

b) Interacts in a relaxed and informal way with students

Children of *all ages* need to know that their teachers care about them as people and as learners. Generally, teachers who demonstrate their genuine concern for their students create classrooms where learning is a positive, successful experience. They have fewer discipline problems and increased achievement.

c) Moves freely among students

Proximity assists in the development of a warm and positive rapport with students. Sitting or standing near students can be particularly beneficial in getting and keeping children's attention. Moving near students is a technique that will help quiet students who are talking or redirect students who are off task.

d) Uses students' names in a warm and friendly way

When someone calls your name in a friendly manner, you are more likely to respond in kind. Adults and children/youth generally are quite similar in this respect. Everyone experiences pleasure from being recognized. Always incorporate children's names into whatever is being taught. Examples should be personalized to students in the classroom.

EXAMPLE:

Suppose John (student in the room) had six cookies. Then Sarah gave him two more. But Leon ate three of them. Using students' names makes content more interesting and may also decrease or eliminate discipline problems. Children listen better when they hear the sound of their names.

Teachers who take the time to build a positive classroom climate reap many benefits and improve student learning.

9. Shows Sensitivity to Needs and Feelings of Students

<table>
<tr><td colspan="5">9.   Shows Sensitivity to Needs and Feelings of Students</td></tr>
<tr><td>①</td><td>②</td><td>③</td><td>④</td><td>⑤</td></tr>
</table>

□   a) Students are reinforced when they do well

□   b) Students are encouraged when they have difficulty

□   c) Students' contributions are accepted in a positive manner

□   d) Students are treated with respect and courtesy

a) Students are reinforced when they do well

Higher student achievement correlates with positive reinforcement. It is important to stress what is right about children's work or behavior rather than be overly concerned about what is wrong with it.

b) Students are encouraged when they have difficulty

Teachers have a tremendous power to influence a child's views of his/her self and often contribute to children's' negative self-image by simply sighing or "head shaking." Teachers who offer positive assurances actually increase students' willingness to try. In addition, teachers who are sensitive to students' feelings actually set children up for success by doing some of the following:

> Have students discuss difficult questions in pairs or triads before asking for individual responses.

> Start a lesson by asking students to think about what they already know about the topic.

> Inform a child who does not know an answer or who has given an incorrect answer that will give him/her a moment for thinking, and that you will come back to him/her again. This technique allows a child to "save face" and experience success instead of failure.

c) Students' contributions are accepted in a positive manner

In any given week, there will be innumerable times that students will give an incorrect response.   Teachers who respond with verbal "putdowns" can stifle interest and growth. Instead, try some of these statements that encourage children to try again.

➢ *That's good thinking, but go further.*

➢ *I like your answer, but think about this one….*

➢ *That's one answer. Can you think of another?*

➢ *You're on the right path.*

➢ *Do you have another idea?*

d) Students are treated with respect and courtesy

An additional component of courtesy is respect – making students feel important.

Example:

If a child arrives in class late and the teacher says angrily, *Where were you? You're late,"* the child may respond in a defensive manner. **Instead** try, *Oh, Bill we are happy to see you!*   When teacher express positive concern instead of angry comments, students are more likely to respond in a positive manner and appropriately modify their behavior.

10.   **Provides Feedback to Students About Behavior**

10.   Provides Feedback to Students About Behavior

①   ②   ③   ④   ⑤

❏   a) Student teacher clearly states expectations about appropriate behavior

❏   b) Student teacher provides verbal feedback for acceptable or unacceptable behavior

❏   c) Student teacher provides non-verbal feedback (smiles, frowns, nods, moves close to student, etc.) for acceptable or unacceptable behavior

❏   d) Student teacher's language is free of derogatory references or sarcasm

a)   Student teacher clearly states expectations about appropriate behavior

Often, management problems develop because teachers assume that children already know how they are expected to act, when in actuality, they really do not understand at all. While most teachers realize the importance of establishing classroom rules, many teachers do not realize the need to *clarify* the rules and to outline specific *expectations*. Likewise, teachers should reinforce expectations quite frequently.

Example:

Bring all needed materials to class. For this rule to be followed, it is important for students to understand expectations. Students should know exactly what supplies to bring, for example, *Students will need to wear their tennis shoes to PE. .*

Respect and be polite to all people. Included under this rule could be listening carefully when anyone is speaking and behaving properly for a substitute.

Respect other people's property This rule might include the following: Keep the room clean and neat, return borrowed property, and ask permission before you use another person's things.

b) **Student teacher provides verbal feedback for acceptable or unacceptable behavior**

The most effective behavioral feedback informs the child specifically how to change inappropriate actions to demonstrate acceptable behavior.

Example: *Katie, I'm glad that you know the answer and are excited about the lesson. But next time you must raise your hand and wait to be called on.*

c) **Student teacher provides nonverbal feedback (smiles, frowns, nods, moves closer to student, etc.) for acceptable or unacceptable behavior**

Because 70% of communication is nonverbal (smiles, frowns, nods, etc.), many effective teachers communicate a large proportion of their behavior management through non-verbal actions.

d) **Student teacher's language is free of derogatory references or sarcasm**

The root word for sarcasm is *sarkaum*. It means *tearing away of the flesh*. Older students may actually enjoy "verbal play" with their teachers — but only when both parties know it is in good humor. When the teacher uses sarcastic statements to discipline, he/she embarrasses the student and rarely changes the behavior.

SPECIAL COACHING TIP: Positive or Negative?

Teachers who consistently reinforce positive behavior have better classroom climates and fewer discipline problems than teachers who focus only on correcting misbehavior. Unfortunately, student teachers have so many details and distractions that they often forget to recognize and consistently affirm positive student behavior.

To double-check your "positive affirmations," it is helpful to conduct a focused observation. Videotape yourself for a 20 to 30 minute time segment. Next, as you observe the tape, tally both the positive reinforcement/affirmation ("Thank you for...", "I appreciate...", "You remembered to..") and the negative comments ("Pay attention.", "Stop ______," and "What did I say?").

Example:

Positive	Negative
III	ⱵⱵ ⱵⱵ I

If the negative comments far exceed the positive affirmations, the student teacher may need to refocus on verbally reinforcing the positive behaviors he/she wants to see.

Remembering to reinforce your students' positive behavior
will actually increase the number of positive actions.

11. Maintains Positive Classroom Behavior

11.   Maintains Positive Classroom Behavior

    ①   ②   ③   ④   ⑤

☐   a) Techniques that help students learn self-management and personal responsibility are utilized

☐   b) Inconsequential behavior problems are overlooked or none exist

☐   c) Appropriate behavior is reinforced

☐   d) Appropriate student behaviors are maintained by maximizing opportunities for each individual to succeed

a)   **Techniques that help students learn self-management and personal responsibility are utilized**

Teachers who work with students to develop a positive classroom community have fewer management problems. Building classroom community is not a simple process and though it takes time to help students become self-monitoring, the effort is a long-term investment in your students' personal development.

b)   **Inconsequential behavior problems are overlooked or none exist**

If there is no audience, it's hard to have a show.

Teachers need to communicate that they know what is going on in the classroom — that they have eyes in the backs of their heads. However, effective teachers recognize that sometimes it is best to ignore minor distractions to stay on task and not to reinforce the disturbances.

Caution: Only ignore inconsequential behaviors. Major behavior problems must be dealt with immediately.

c)   **Appropriate behavior is reinforced**

Teachers should "catch" children behaving appropriately and reinforce these behaviors. When a behavior is reinforced, it increases the likelihood that the student will repeat that behavior in the future.   Many successful teachers reinforce students for following rules rather than for breaking them.

A majority of student teachers express concern over managing disruptive student behavior. *An ounce of prevention…* the saying goes. Taking steps to encourage "good" behavior is easier than controlling disruptive behavior. It is important to recognize and "reward" positive behavior for individuals as well as groups. How students are recognized and what rewards are appropriate will vary with ages and groups.

Remember, nonverbal recognition and rewards are just as powerful as verbal or material reinforcement.

Guidelines for reinforcing behavior:

> ➢   **Praise positive behavior.** Offer specific, immediate feedback.

> ➢   **Be specific by naming the behavior.** *"Thank you for doing…"*

> ➢   **Be consistent!** If teachers want students to behave, they must be consistent. A consistent, predictable world makes for more predictable, well-behaved students.

d)   **Appropriate student behaviors are maintained by maximizing opportunities for each individual to succeed**

Students of all ages who are failing classroom learning tasks are very likely to act out their frustrations by becoming disruptive. Teachers can increase the likelihood of positive student behavior if they make sure students are learning materials at a high rate of success. Another bonus: Students tend to continue to learn more if they are working at an 80% plus success rate.

12. Manages Disruptive Behavior

<u>All</u> teachers have to deal with disruptive behavior,
but how often depends on how the teacher handles the disruptions.

---

12.   Manages Disruptive Behavior

      ①   ②   ③   ④   ⑤

❑   a) Individuals who have caused disruptions are dealt with rather than the entire class being punished

❑   b) Major disruptions are attended to quickly and appropriately

❑   c) Consequences for misbehavior are based on the severity of the disruption

❑   d) Disruptive behavior rarely occurs

---

a)   Individuals who have caused disruptions are dealt with rather than the entire class being punished

Sometimes peer pressure can be helpful in persuading students to behave the way we want them to behave. *However,* if the whole class is punished when only one individual breaks the rule, even very young children become resentful toward the teacher.

b)   Major disruptions are attended to quickly and appropriately

Effective consequences must be immediate, occurring after the inappropriate behavior. It is also important to be consistent in responding to student behavior. A teacher who is not consistent in attending to discipline problems may actually see misbehavior increase.

c)   Consequences for misbehavior are based on the severity of the disruption

Experienced classroom teachers suggest student teachers consider the range of consequences for potential problems. Likewise, veteran teachers encourage new teachers to "count to 10" before assigning a consequence. This "count" helps to keep new teachers from overreacting to discipline problems.

d)   **Disruptive behavior rarely occurs**

Effective teachers use a number of proactive techniques to establish and maintain a positive classroom community. The following examples are just a few suggestions.

> ➢   Stand by the door as children enter the classroom.

> ➢   Have something for the children to do as soon as they arrive at their desks or as soon as they've finished an activity or assignment. Many effective teachers provide a routine for students to follow every day when they arrive in class. Such a task settles children and enables the teacher or students to take care of routine matters, such as attendance.

> ➢   "The look," a quiet, but powerful management tool is often sufficient to stop such offenses as pencil tapping, paper rattling, inappropriate chatting, etc.

> ➢   Deliver a soft reminder. A quiet reminder will not cause a major disruption or attract the negative attention the student might want for the sake of impressing peers.

> ➢   Proximity-control – Move near a disturbance instead of trying to stop it from a distance.

(Adapted from Edmund T. Emmer, 1982)

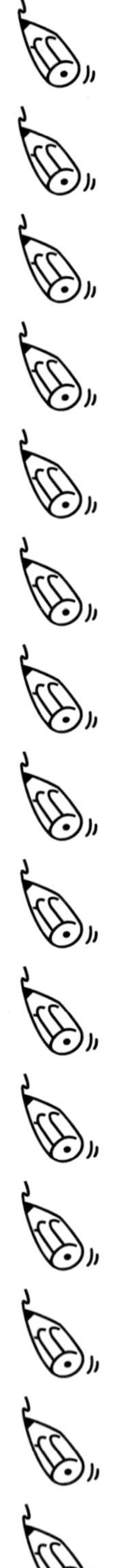

NOTES

Implements and Manages Instruction and Assessment

Excellent instructional delivery is an art that improves with time, practice and effort.

Research support for this chapter includes: Baumann, 1988; Berliner & Casanova, 1993; Brophy & Good, 1986; Comber & Nichols, 2004; Duffy & Roehler, 1986; French, 2004; Gage & Berliner, 1984; Gagne, 1985; Good, Li, 2006; Lobman, 2006; Lybolt, Armstrong, Evans & Gottfred, 2007; Slavings & Mason, 1988; Hunter, 1982; Levin & Lang, 1981; Morine-Dershimer & Beyerbach, 1987; Morrow, 2007; Olness, 2007; Ornstein, 1988; Rosenshine & Stevens, 1986; Rowe, 1969 and 1986; Stiggins, 1986; Terpstra & Tamura, 2008; Wilen, 1986.

13.   **Begins Lesson Effectively**

<table>
<tr><td colspan="6">13.   Begins Lesson Effectively</td></tr>
<tr><td></td><td>①</td><td>②</td><td>③</td><td>④</td><td>⑤</td></tr>
<tr><td>❑</td><td colspan="5">a) Student teacher activates/establishes students' prior knowledge of current lesson</td></tr>
<tr><td>❑</td><td colspan="5">b) Student teacher helps students to understand the purpose or importance of the lesson</td></tr>
<tr><td>❑</td><td colspan="5">c) Student teacher links new information to students' existing knowledge</td></tr>
<tr><td>❑</td><td colspan="5">d) Student teacher stimulates interest in lesson by actively involving students or by asking thought-provoking questions</td></tr>
</table>

What the teacher does in the first few minutes of the lesson is essential for motivating students' interest and setting the "stage" for learning.

a)   Student teacher activates/establishes students' prior knowledge of current lesson

What can you tell me about ________________?

When children are asked to reveal what they already know about a topic, it helps the teacher to determine how much background knowledge must be provided to help students understand the new information being presented.

b)   Student teacher helps students to understand the purpose or importance of the lesson

A good introduction, often called an anticipatory set, helps children become ready to learn. A good lesson introduction:

➢   gets the learners' attention,
➢   often involves overt participation,
➢   connects prior knowledge to new information,
➢   helps the student learn faster, and
➢   reduces discipline problems.

c) **Student teacher links new information to students' existing knowledge**

If the teacher associates something that the children already know or understand with the new content, the students will be likely to feel more confident and thus more likely to want to learn.

d) **Student teacher stimulates interest in lesson by actively involving students or by asking thought-provoking questions**

Questions stimulate children's interest, activate prior knowledge, and encourage children to develop their own questions about the topic being discussed.

Examples of good introductions:

Raise your hand if you have ever had a bad day? How did you feel? Today we are going to read a story about a little boy named Alexander, who is having a terrible, horrible, no good, very bad day.

How many scoops of ice cream will it take to fill up this bowl? I want to buy enough ice cream for the Friday afternoon class party. How would I begin to figure out how many scoops I will need to buy?

Starting the lesson successfully requires more than "turn to page…"

14. Presents Information Clearly

<table>
<tr><td colspan="5">14.   Presents Information Clearly</td></tr>
<tr><td>①</td><td>②</td><td>③</td><td>④</td><td>⑤</td></tr>
</table>

❑   a) Student teacher directly relates information to desired learner outcomes

❑   b) Student teacher presents information in a logical sequence

❑   c) Student teacher provides concrete and/or visual models when appropriate

❑   d) Student teacher uses vocabulary appropriate to students' level of understanding

a)   Student teacher directly relates information to desired learner outcomes

When children are learning something for the first time, information that the teacher presents should be correlated with the desired outcomes. Teachers need to thoughtfully consider how information is presented to the learner. It is particularly important to teach directly to an outcome/objective:

➢   when students are first introduced to a concept,

➢   when the information is complicated, and

➢   when students are having difficulty learning.

b)   Student teacher presents information in a logical sequence

Though learning is not always step-by-step progression, knowledge does build upon prior information. When lessons build from known to new, from simple to complex, the teacher increases the likelihood that children will learn and retain the information presented.

c) **Student teacher provides concrete and/or visual models when appropriate**

It is important that all children have access to learning information. Visual models or samples are provided so that every child has an opportunity to use multiple modalities to learn successfully.

d) **Student teacher uses vocabulary appropriate to students' level of understanding**

Using words that clarify instead of confuse is essential to learning. It is also useful to visually connect old vocabulary to new. This technique is called semantic webbing or mapping.

Presenting information in a clear manner requires thoughtful planning and effective delivery.

15. Gives Clear Directions and Explanations

<table>
<tr><td colspan="6">15. Gives Clear Directions and Explanations</td></tr>
<tr><td></td><td>①</td><td>②</td><td>③</td><td>④</td><td>⑤</td></tr>
<tr><td>❑</td><td colspan="5">a) Student teacher presents directions in a logical sequence</td></tr>
<tr><td>❑</td><td colspan="5">b) Student teacher writes critical information on board, chart, or overhead</td></tr>
<tr><td>❑</td><td colspan="5">c) Student teacher clearly informs students what they should be doing, where to do it, and for how long</td></tr>
<tr><td>❑</td><td colspan="5">d) Student teacher checks students' understanding of directions before they practice independently</td></tr>
</table>

Clear directions and instructions help students learn successfully and minimize confusion and discouragement. When students receive clear directions, they understand what the teacher wants them to do. The skill of giving clear and precise directions and explanations must be acquired and practiced.

a) Student teacher presents directions in a logical sequence

b) Student teacher writes critical information on board, chart, or overhead

> ➢ Puts assignments on the board where all the children can see them.

> ➢ Makes a transparency of worksheet and uses overhead projector to demonstrate correct process.

c) Student teacher clearly informs students what they should be doing, where to do it, and for how long

For example,

Children, we are going to be working in our centers for the next 20 minutes. When you hear the signal, it will be time to clean up our centers and return to circle.

We are going to be starting writer's workshop for the next hour. I'm going to provide a 10-minute lesson on using quotation marks since many of you are writing character dialogue.

d)   Student teacher checks students' understanding of directions before they practice independently

> Asks children to repeat directions or main ideas.

> Makes clear the requirements and grading criteria/rubric for each assignment.

> Checks children's work and assignments daily. Even if the students check their own or each other's work, the student teacher should collect homework and look for errors or misunderstandings.

> Circulates quickly and looks at the children's work.

> Whenever children begin any seatwork assignments, student teacher walks by each student to be sure he or she is able to do the work correctly.

> When possible, begins seatwork together as a class. Working together enables the student teacher and children to uncover possible confusion about the assignment.

> When children are at work, the student teacher should frequently walk around the classroom to check progress. This will help to keep students on task as well as provide assistance for those who need it.

Writing multistep directions is a good way of keeping children on task.

16.   Uses Student Responses and Questions in Teaching

16.   Uses Student Responses and Questions in Teaching

① ② ③ ④ ⑤

❑   a) Student teacher encourages students' responses and/or questions

❑   b) Student teacher responds in a positive and supportive manner

❑   c) Student teacher incorporates student responses and questions into the lesson

❑   d) Student teacher uses responses to monitor student understanding of information presented

a)   Student teacher encourages students' responses and/or questions

When children are encouraged to ask questions and give responses during a lesson, they are more likely to be motivated to stay on task and learn throughout the entire lesson.

b)   Student teacher responds in a positive and supportive manner

Responds positively both ***verbally***

➢   *Good question.*

➢   *Thank-you for asking that.*

and ***nonverbally***

➢   *smiling*

➢   *nodding head*

➢   *active listening*

c)   **Student teacher incorporates student responses and questions into the lesson**

When teachers incorporate children's responses and questions into the lesson, student motivation and interest are increased. However, in attempting to relate students' ideas to the lesson, the teacher should not allow irrelevant ideas to take the focus off the main idea of the lesson.

d)   **Student teacher uses responses to monitor student understanding of information presented**

To the perceptive teacher, children's questions serve as a mirror, reflecting their level of understanding of the lesson. Student questions pinpoint areas of confusion and allow the teacher to adjust the instruction rapidly.

When the teacher positively reinforces student involvement, students are more likely to participate.

17.   Maximizes Opportunities for All to Participate

<table>
<tr><td colspan="5">17.   Maximizes Opportunities for All to Participate</td></tr>
<tr><td>①</td><td>②</td><td>③</td><td>④</td><td>⑤</td></tr>
</table>

❑   a) Student teacher asks questions of whole group first, rather than individuals

❑   b) Student teacher provides appropriate wait-time for all students after asking questions and redirects accordingly

❑   c) Student teacher offers frequent opportunities for student-to-student interactions/inquiry

❑   d) Student teacher provides opportunities for covert/overt participation, such as physical movement, manipulations, small group activities, discussions, and/or debates

Studies reveal that students remember:

10% of what they read
20% of what they hear
30% of what they see
50% of what they see and hear
70% of what they say
90% of what they say while doing

Active Participation — Children who actively participate in a lesson tend to be more accountable, responsible, and successful than students who are merely bystanders. Children should actively participate throughout the *entire* lesson.

a)   Student teacher asks questions of whole group first, then individuals

Covert Participation means that children are actively involved in nonobservable behaviors. When teachers ask students to think, recall, or imagine, it increases the chances that students will actually become mentally involved. When students think before they answer out loud, the quality of their answers improves.

Asking a question first and **then** calling a child's name is an effective method teachers can use to keep all students mentally involved. When the question comes before the child's name, the teacher causes all students to begin thinking and processing their answers, thus keeping all students involved.

b) **Student teacher provides appropriate wait-time for all students after asking questions and redirects accordingly**

Wait-time is the interval between the teacher's question and the child's response. Wait-time is a form of covert involvement. The average teacher waits less than one second before giving up on one child and going on to the next. Students need time to think. When teachers stretch out wait-time to even three seconds, children's rates of correct responses and more verbally complex sentences dramatically improves.

Teachers should use questioning techniques that allow all students an opportunity to participate and respond successfully. Asking a question and then allowing students to discuss it with a study buddy before they respond is an excellent way to keep all students engaged and achieving.

c) **Student teacher offers frequent opportunities for student-to-student interactions/inquiry**

Child-to-child discussions encourage whole class participation and typically intensify students' interest in the topic.

d) **Student teacher provides opportunities for covert/overt participation, such as physical movement, manipulations, small group activities, discussions and/or debates**

Overt involvement from students simultaneously provides the teacher with measurable, observable evidence of students' progress.

Examples:

> *Write answers on scratch pad.*

> *Talk it over with a neighbor.*

> *Raise your hand if….*

> *Thumbs up if you agree, down if you disagree.*

When attempting to involve children in a lesson, it is important to make **all children** feel accountable for thinking, working, doing, and participating – **throughout the entire lesson.**

18. Provides Students Feedback Throughout Lesson

<table>
<tr><td colspan="5">18. Provides Students Feedback Throughout Lesson</td></tr>
<tr><td>①</td><td>②</td><td>③</td><td>④</td><td>⑤</td></tr>
</table>

❑ a) Student teacher provides feedback to students as soon as possible

❑ b) Student teacher provides feedback to students in a positive manner

❑ c) Student teacher specifically tells students/parents about the strengths and weaknesses in student performance and gives suggestions on how performance can be improved

❑ d) Student teacher helps students evaluate their own performance

a) Student teacher provides feedback to students as soon as possible

Children can learn and practice mistakes as easily as correct information. Frequently checking students' understanding provides the teacher immediate information that reveals what concepts students understand or misinterpret.

Hint: Grading papers can become time-consuming and overwhelming. Not all assignments need to be assessed by the teacher. In addition to self-assessment, students may use pair-checking, then peer tutoring, with the teacher providing support.

b) Student teacher provides feedback to students in a positive manner

When children don't understand, the teacher needs to determine the source of the confusion and reteach the concept in a friendly, supportive manner. Comments like *You should have paid more attention* or *You're not listening* work against the goal of successful learning and active participation by causing students to become defensive.

c) **Student teacher specifically tells students/parents about the strengths and weaknesses in student performance and gives suggestions on how performance can be improved**

Feedback to children on the level of their performance should be as specific as possible. Specific means: *The child is told what is right about the performance, what is wrong about it, and how it can be improved.* Informing the student what he/she did right reinforces the student and increases the chance that the correct performance will occur again.

Examples:

Instead of*: "You're doing fine."*

Try: *"You've come up with a good example of a rhyme, and if you check the last four letters….yes, that is right the letters are the same. "*

Instead of: *"No, that's wrong. Try again."*

Try: *"You have the first one correct, except ________________. I'll come back in a minute and check the next one."*

It is also important for teachers to keep parents informed about student progress. Parents need to understand how their child's progress is assessed and specifically how parents can support their student's learning efforts.

d) **Student teacher helps students evaluate their own performance**

Teachers need to help students develop specific performance criteria and teach them how to evaluate their own performance.

Example:

A primary multi-age teacher and her class were discussing qualities of fluent oral reading. The teacher played three examples of one child reading the same text. The class noticed that during the first reading the child had great difficulty pronouncing the words. During the second oral reading the class recognized the student had improved and now could read all the words easily, but did not pay attention to the punctuation marks. As the class listened to the third reading, they realized that the child was reading fluently, with expression, and paid attention to the punctuation marks. As the children discussed the problems related to the first two readings, they also shared ideas for improving these oral-reading skills. During the discussion the teacher wrote the oral reading rubric and then listed the children's suggestions for improving oral reading. (Enz & Serafini, 1995).

19. Instruction Promotes Student Retention and Understanding

19.   Instruction Promotes Student Retention and Understanding

    ①   ②   ③   ④   ⑤

❑   a) Student teacher uses techniques which help to make material relevant to students and explains the importance of the lesson

❑   b) Student teacher defines or models the expectations of the lesson or learning

❑   c) Student teacher provides opportunities for all students to demonstrate an understanding of what is being taught

❑   d) Student teacher monitors student responses, interprets the source of student errors, and adjusts instruction accordingly

a)   Student teacher uses techniques which help to make material relevant to students and explains the importance of the lesson

Most people pay better attention and remember longer when they believe the information being presented is relevant or interesting.

Examples:

How do you know if we need to stop at a street? That is right, we will see a stop sign! Today we are going to begin to learn about traffic signs. We are going to practice our safety obstacle course. .

Who likes peanut butter and jelly sandwiches? Have you ever had a peanut butter and jelly mixture that was too much jelly and not enough peanut butter? Today we are going to learn about ratios. Ratios will help you make the perfect blend of peanut butter and jelly.

b) **Student teacher defines or models the expectations of the lesson or learning**

On those occasions when children must demonstrate specific behaviors, the teacher provides a model of "how it should be." The likelihood of success is increased because students have seen the correct performance and are aware of the specific part(s).

For example:

* How to line up for recess

* How to "log on" to a computer

When precise performance is expected, it becomes important to label exactly which part of the model is critical to successful performance.

* *This example is correct; because margins are 1 inch.*

* *The students who just lined up for recess did it correctly, because they…*

c) **Student teacher provides opportunities for all students to demonstrate an understanding of what is being taught**

Guided Practice: Guided practice is practice that occurs during initial stages of learning. In guided practice, students practice under teacher supervision.

Independent Practice: Independent practice may occur when the teacher has observed that every student demonstrates an understanding of the concepts. Independent practice, such as homework, needs to be practice of the *same skill* that has already been practiced correctly under supervision. Asking children to practice a skill they do not know how to do or that has not yet been taught is inappropriate.

d) **Student teacher monitors student responses, interprets the source of student errors, and adjust instruction accordingly**

Monitoring student responses enables the teacher to catch student errors and provide appropriate feedback so mistakes are not practiced. Likewise, monitoring children's performance reveals how the students perceived the teacher's instruction.

20.   Uses Effective Closure or Summarization Techniques

<table>
<tr><td colspan="5">20.   Uses Effective Closure or Summarization Techniques</td></tr>
<tr><td>①</td><td>②</td><td>③</td><td>④</td><td>⑤</td></tr>
</table>

❑   a) Student teacher gives students an opportunity for closure/summarization at the end of distinct segments within the lesson or between objectives

❑   b) Student teacher provides opportunity for the students to summarize at the end of each lesson

❑   c) Student teacher actively involves students in their own closure/summarization

❑   d) Student teacher extends closure/summarization to future applications or actions

a)   Student teacher gives students an opportunity for closure or summarization at the end of distinct segments within the lesson or between objectives

b)   Student teacher provides opportunity for the students to summarize at the end of each lesson

Research suggests that most people learn more quickly and remember what they have learned when they summarize the major elements presented. This is especially important when the lesson has a number of critical steps.

Examples of Closure:

Write or tell your neighbor three things that you learned about…

Let's all go through the process one more time.

Jot down the steps in the scientific process.

c)   **Student teacher actively involves students in their own closure or summarization**

As discussed earlier, children remember information longer if they are actively involved. Since closure helps to *cement the learning*, it makes sense to involve students in the closure process.

d)   **Student teacher extends closure/summarization to future applications or actions**

Children of all ages like to know the information they learn today will be useful in what they'll learn tomorrow. Closure can serve to make this connection in their minds.

Examples:

Today we discussed the major parts of the life cycle of a butterfly. Can you name them?

Tomorrow we will learn about the body parts of the butterfly.

Teaching Hint: Closure is a significant part of any lesson. However, beginning teachers frequently experience difficulty with lesson closure. In most cases, the closure activity was not clearly delineated when the lesson plan was developed. It is important for teachers to plan a lesson closure with the same effort used to plan a lesson opening.

Likewise, poor pacing can contribute to closure problems, as many teachers just "run out of time." Experienced teachers appear to have developed an "internal clock" that helps them pace lessons with sufficient time for closure activities. New teachers may wish to set a timer to ring 10-minutes prior to the end of a period to allow adequate time to present a well-planned closure activity.

21.   Uses Instructional Material Effectively

<table>
<tr><td colspan="5">21.   Uses Instructional Material Effectively</td></tr>
<tr><td>①</td><td>②</td><td>③</td><td>④</td><td>⑤</td></tr>
</table>

❑   a) Student teacher uses instructional equipment and other aids, such as charts, graphs, overhead, video, slides, software, maps, and/or manipulatives

❑   b) Student teacher uses instructional resources that contribute to the students' understanding of lesson goals/objectives

❑   c) Student teacher smoothly blends media with other types of instruction

❑   d) Student teacher creates original instructional aids which are relevant and enhance the effectiveness of teaching

When teachers use various types of instructional materials, media, models, etc., they make instruction more exciting, meaningful, and effective. However, instructional materials/models must be directly related to the desired learning outcome.

Example:

A student teacher brought a chart of the circulatory system to begin her science lesson. Unfortunately, the topic being studied was the skeleton. Obviously, the children in that class were confused.

Hint: Mentor teachers have collected resource materials for years and have had many opportunities to learn how to use these resources most effectively. New teachers need guidance in locating, selecting, and using the most appropriate instructional materials.

In addition to many resources,...

Sunny Atkinson, 1984

22. Promotes Individual Student Learning

22. Promotes Individual Student Learning

①   ②   ③   ④   ⑤

❑   a) Materials chosen are directly related to the goals/objectives of the lesson

❑   b) Materials selected ensure appropriate level of student success

❑   c) Students are given ample opportunity to use materials as intended

❑   d) Students' interaction with the materials is monitored to determine their understanding

a) Materials chosen are directly related to the goals/objectives of the lesson

Practice should be designed to develop fluency and broaden the understanding of the content. Practice should be focused on the content being practiced.

b) Materials selected ensure appropriate level of student success

Independent, *in-school* practice needs to be carefully considered. Students who are successfully practicing are eager to continue learning. Likewise, practicing a mistake makes remediation extremely difficult and practice beyond the point of mastery decreases motivation. Homework and independent, *in-school* work should be assigned only after the child has demonstrated ability to perform the skill with minimal errors.

c) Students are given ample opportunity to use materials as intended

This is especially important when the teacher is using any type of manipulative materials. Teachers need to be sure there are sufficient materials so that all children have an opportunity to use materials; likewise, children need time to explore, discover, and analyze.

d)   **Students' interaction with the materials is monitored to determine their understanding**

Frequent monitoring of children's progress cannot be overemphasized. When students learn information incorrectly, they become extremely frustrated and subsequent learning is delayed.

The following questions may be helpful in determining if the instructional materials selected are appropriate:

➢   Does the practice assignment accomplish desired learner outcomes?

➢   Is the outcome worth accomplishing?

➢   Have the children demonstrated the skills/knowledge necessary for success?

➢   Is the most learning being realized for the time spent?

➢   Can the assignment be completed without thinking or by guessing?

➢   Is the paper legible?

➢   Are the directions and vocabulary comprehensible to the children?

➢   Is the number of examples/problems/questions appropriate?

➢   Are maximal inspiration and minimal perspiration required by the teacher in creating and correcting the assignment?

23. Uses Teaching Methods Appropriately/Effectively

Children have individual needs and diverse learning styles. A number of research studies have shown that when teachers use a variety of methodologies/techniques, the quality of instruction improves and school becomes more interesting for students and teachers.

There is no one best way for children to learn. The teacher must consider a variety of methods that would offer the greatest opportunity for students to explore, experience, and ultimately learn. Teachers should use multimodality approaches, as a variety of approaches will best meet the needs of all students in the room.

The following descriptors provide suggestions for the student teacher to consider when planning and presenting instruction:

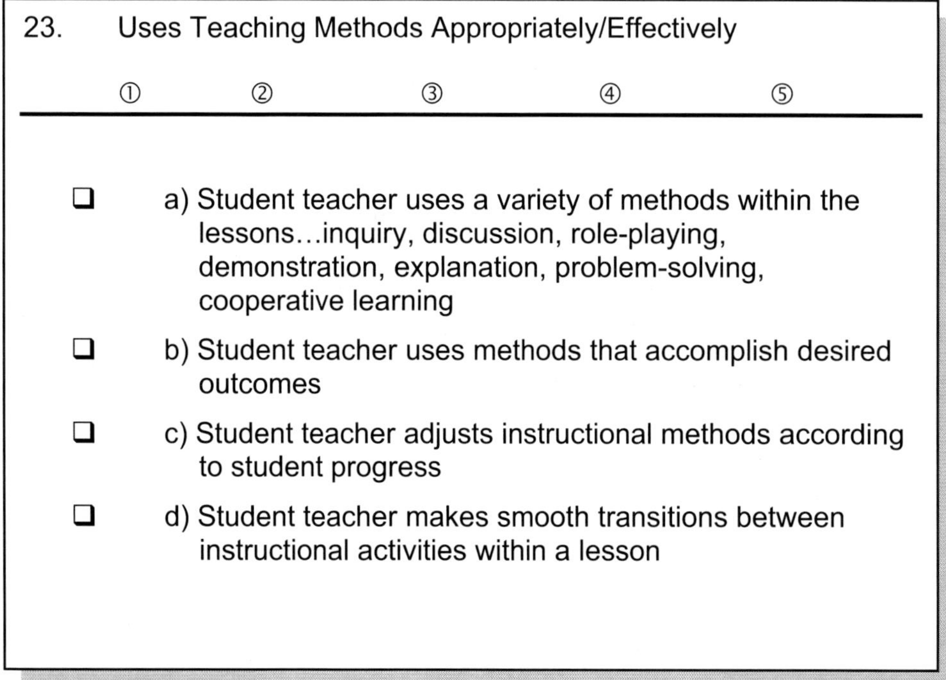

When multiple presentation strategies are offered in a particular lesson, it becomes exciting for the students. However, if transitions are not carefully planned, a great deal of instructional learning time may be lost. To prevent a great lesson from becoming lost time, teachers need to also plan for student movement and for its effective management.

Instructional Approaches Review

Review your lesson plans for the week, focusing attention on the types of instructional activities/learning strategies planned. Place a check in the box and include the approximate amount of time planned for this strategy.

Approach	M	T	W	Th	F
Discovery Lesson					
5 E Inquiry Lesson					
Discussion: - **Teacher-led** - **Student-led**					
Role-playing					
Demonstration: - **Teacher-led** - **Student-led**					
Explanation: - **Teacher-led** - **Student-led**					
Problem Solving					
Cooperative Learning					

If only one or two strategies are checked, especially those that require students to sit quietly and listen, then the opportunity for <u>all</u> learners to be successful is greatly reduced.

24.   Uses Instructional Time Effectively

<table>
<tr><td>24.</td><td colspan="5">Uses Instructional Time Effectively</td></tr>
<tr><td></td><td>①</td><td>②</td><td>③</td><td>④</td><td>⑤</td></tr>
</table>

☐   a) Activities begin on schedule

☐   b) Allocated instructional time is maximized

☐   c) Instructional pacing is appropriate for students

☐   d) There are no significant delays or periods of time during which the students are not effectively engaged

a)   Activities begin on schedule

b)   Allocated instructional time is maximized

Research has demonstrated that effective teachers use instructional time wisely.

SPONGE ACTIVITIES: Transitions between activities, classes, or periods are a major source of lost time. In the average classroom, one hour a day is lost in transitions. This adds up to five hours a week. Statements and directives such as the following will reduce time lost in transition. Sponge activities can be used to minimize wasted time.

Example:

When the students first enter the room, before the bell has rung:

➢   *On your paper, write three things that you remember from yesterday.*

➢   *Read the first page of the story and think of a question to ask a friend.*

As the teacher or student helper passes out the materials:

➢   *Students, be thinking about _____________. When you get your book, look on page _____ to see if you're right.*

➢   *Think of a question about _____________.*

c)   **Instructional pacing is appropriate for students**

It is important to remember that not all children work at the same pace. This fact is a source of great frustration for most teachers. Try using differential assignments for the range of student abilities. Core assignments with optional choices may also be a useful technique to help manage students and time.

d)   **There are no significant delays or periods of time during which the students are not effectively engaged**

SPECIAL COACHING TIP: To determine if instructional time is being used efficiently, teachers should observe themselves via videotape. As the teacher observes the taped lesson, he/she can provide answers to the following statements:

Yes	No	N/A	Student Teacher Actions
			1. Teacher greets students, family members as they enter the classroom
			2. Students complete transition routines, such as attendance and lunch choices, and turning in paperwork.
			3. The environment is prepared and ready for students. Instructional materials/supplies are immediately available.
			4. Student(s) quickly transition to learning activities.
			5. Clear, logical, sequenced directions are given only when teacher has students' attention.
			6. Complex directions are broken down and given separately.
			7. Teacher physically circulates and regularly visually scans whole room.
			8. Any guidance is given with a direct, friendly tone and posture.
			9. Transition from one activity to another is smooth, taking less than two minutes.
			10. All students are experiencing a high rate of success throughout the lesson.

NOTE: If three or more statements are marked "no," the teacher may not be using instructional time efficiently.

25. Demonstrates Knowledge of Subject

<table>
<tr><td colspan="6">25.   Demonstrates Knowledge of Subject</td></tr>
<tr><td></td><td>①</td><td>②</td><td>③</td><td>④</td><td>⑤</td></tr>
<tr><td>❏</td><td colspan="5">a) Student teacher's subject area knowledge is accurate and current</td></tr>
<tr><td>❏</td><td colspan="5">b) Information and materials present concepts and ideas in multiple ways</td></tr>
<tr><td>❏</td><td colspan="5">c) Student teacher asks higher-order questions and/or builds on students' questions</td></tr>
<tr><td>❏</td><td colspan="5">d) Student teacher is enthusiastic about content area and is able to involve or motivate students in subject matter</td></tr>
</table>

a)   **Student teacher's subject area knowledge is accurate and current**

Effective teachers possess a comprehensive knowledge of their content.

b)   **Information and materials present concepts and ideas in multiple ways**

When teachers provide interesting stories and facts about the topic that go beyond the confines of the text, they increase the students' understanding of the content.

c)   **Student teacher asks higher-order questions and/or builds on students' questions**

A comprehensive knowledge of the topic gives the confidence to examine difficult concepts and challenge students' thinking.

d)   **Student teacher is enthusiastic about content area and is able to involve or motivate students in subject matter**

Enthusiasm is contagious. Many unmotivated students have been inspired to actually become singers, mathematicians, scientists, writers, etc., because of the direct influence of a dedicated teacher.

26.   Manages Conditions for Teaching and Learning

26.   Manages Conditions for Teaching and Learning

    ①   ②   ③   ④   ⑤

❑   a) Basic management skills are implemented to efficiently and effectively instruct the class: instructional tools are readily accessible

❑   b) Student interactions are facilitated by room arrangements

❑   c) Routine tasks are handled smoothly by teacher and/or students (attendance, lunch count, etc.)

❑   d) Materials and supplies are readily available; distribution and collection of materials have been planned

In every classroom there are hundreds of tasks that must be performed daily. How the teacher manages these tasks impacts his/her overall teaching effectiveness. When both children and teachers have a clear understanding of expected procedures, instructional time is likely to be used effectively. Students will be likely to stay on task – increasing the amount of instruction provided and decreasing behavior problems that result from students who are not actively involved in the instructional process.

Procedures for Beginning Class

What routine tasks need efficient handling at the beginning of the period?
The student teacher handles or delegates to children such tasks as attendance as quickly and efficiently as possible.

When the bell rings, what are students supposed to do?
When the bell rings, most teachers expect children to listen. A regular beginning class routine for the first four or five minutes of class is a good idea. Students should begin the activity as soon as the bell rings.

Procedures During Instruction

How will students seek the teacher's help if they have question?
Teachers should call on nonvolunteers. Most teachers require children to raise their hands to ask a question. When students are working at their seats and need help, they are asked to raise their hands so the student teacher can go to them. This will avoid long lines or noisy groups by the teacher's desk. It will allow the teacher to control when and where to give individual assistance.

Under what conditions may students leave their seats (to sharpen pencils, turn in papers, etc.)?
To eliminate unnecessary wandering around the room, many teachers indicate when and why students are allowed to leave their seats. For example, students may sharpen pencils before class only.

Under what conditions will students leave the room and go to the bathroom or other locations?
This procedure must be established early in the semester and consistently followed throughout the year. Most teachers do not allow children to leave the room except in emergencies, as determined by the teacher. Many teachers feel the passing period or recess is normally sufficient time for going to restrooms, lockers, etc.

What signal will the teacher use to get the students' attention?
Some of the techniques used by teachers are a timer, bell, turning on the lights, sitting down by the overhead projector, standing by the chalkboard, or a particular phrase, such as "Let me have your attention." It is helpful to consistently use a particular signal that will let students know you are ready to begin a presentation or lesson.

Will student talk to one another and/or work together during class?
If this will be allowed, the student teacher will need to establish specific limitations. For example, during certain activities, quiet talking will be allowed. But if the talking gets too loud, the privilege will be lost. If quiet talking or cooperative learning is allowed, monitoring is still necessary.

How will students work at centers or engage in self-paced activities?
If there are enrichment activities for faster-working students, it will need to be specified exactly when these materials may be used, how many students may be involved in any single activity, where the materials will be kept, and what the procedures are for returning materials to their places.

Procedures for Ending Class

What procedures are needed for putting away supplies/equipment?
Leave enough time for students to put everything away and to pick up things in their area. If class monitors are to do anything other than pass out or pick up materials, the teacher will need to have specific instructions for them. If students return materials or supplies individually, the teacher might appoint a student monitor who has the responsibility of checking to be sure all materials have been returned.

How can teaching materials, supplies and student papers be organized?
Do not let the papers, materials, or records from different periods or subjects get jumbled together. Use file folders, boxes, baskets, etc. to store things.

What standards of neatness are required before dismissing the class?
The student teacher should expect students to leave the room as clean as it was when they came in. Students should check around their chairs for paper or other trash.

What procedures will be used to dismiss the class?
Most effective teachers require all students to be in their seats and quiet before they may be dismissed. Because students do not want to be dismissed late, they will generally respond quickly if this requirement is enforced.

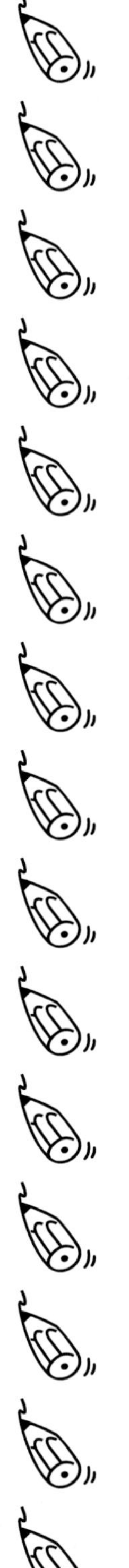

NOTES

```
Chapter 5

Best Advice: A University Supervisor's Perspective
```

Student teaching provides a number challenges – both personally and professionally. This chapter quickly reviews student teaching requirements and offers many helpful suggestions offered by experienced university supervisors. The information is organized in a sequential manner that closely follows the Phase-In Schedule described on pages 22-24 and the Developmental Planning charts on pages 7-9.

Before the semester begins, the student teacher should

> ➢ Visit the mentor teacher as many times as possible.

> ➢ Closely observe the mentor's classroom management techniques, classroom routines and procedure, (see Enz, B.J., Kortman, S., & Honaker, C. *Managing the Primary and Elementary Classroom.* Kendall-Hunt Publishers, Dubuque, IA. and review Observation Guide and Orientation Activities (pages 14-18).

> ➢ Attend student teaching orientation. Purchase and bring *The Dual Certification Student Teaching Experience and Coaching the Special Education Student Teacher (Dual Certification)* to the meeting. At the orientation you will meet with the university supervisor, who will review requirements and discuss concerns and expectations.

Important Expectation:

Dress professionally. First impressions are powerful and lasting. Students, supervisors, and professional staff make decisions regarding a student teacher's professional competence based on appearance and demeanor.

Phase I — Observation to Partial Responsibility

During the *first days* of the apprenticeship, the student teacher should
- share complete contact information (home, cell telephone numbers, and email) with your mentor teacher,

- share companion text, *Coaching the Special Education Student Teacher (Dual Certification)*, with the mentor teacher. This text contains all the forms the mentor teacher will need throughout the semester,

- review and complete the Developmental Planning Chart that clarifies the time frame for gradually assuming teaching responsibilities and helps to delineate the subjects and content to be taught this semester (see pages 8-9 for examples of completed Developmental Planning Charts.),

- complete and discuss, with your mentor teacher, the Student Teaching Questionnaire on pages 10-13,

- organize the student teaching notebook (see pages 43-44.), and

- arrange for your supervisor's first visit.

Hints:

With the help of the mentor, establish an organized workspace and become informed where basic teaching supplies are kept.

In addition to school supplies, student teachers may wish to bring any medications and personal items, such as antihistamines, pain relievers, antiseptic hand gel, tissues, etc. (NOTE: It is important to follow school procedures for storing these items.)

*****Call or e-mail the University Supervisor with any concerns or questions.*****

By the *beginning of the second week,* the student teacher should

> ➢ complete Observation Guide and Orientation Activities (see pages 15-20),

> ➢ complete first-week timecard information (see pages 34-36),

> ➢ participate in your supervisor's online discussion group,

> ➢ write first weekly reflection entry (see pages 31-33),

> ➢ establish ONE calendar that contains both personal and professional commitments and due dates, and

> ➢ learn student's names, begin to observe their behavior patterns and assess learning needs. see Enz, B.J., Kortman, S., & Honaker, C. *Managing the Primary and Elementary Classroom.* Kendall-Hunt Publishers, Dubuque, IA provides a number of "Get Acquainted" activities.

Hint:

Review your calendar at least twice daily and add updated information in pencil. Be sure to note student teaching requirements, such as seminars, workshops, trimester progress report due dates, parent-teacher conferences, report-card/grading term, supervisor's visits, and personal commitments.

Calendar

Sunday	Monday	Tuesday	Wednesday	Thursday	Friday	Saturday

Your calendar will become your constant companion.

Call or email the University Supervisor with any concerns or questions.

During Phase II, student teachers should:

➢ become familiar with faculty, staff, and school environment, and learn about district policies and school-wide procedures,

➢ observe mentor teacher's instruction strategies (Observation Guide, pages 15-20),

➢ ask the mentor to complete Weekly Progress Forms (in companion text, *Coaching the Special Education Student Teacher (Dual Certification),*

➢ gather instructional resources, develop lesson plans and slowly assume teaching responsibilities

➢ attend seminars and maintain notebook, lesson plans, weekly reflection entries, online discussions, and timecard,

➢ arrange supervisor's first observation, and

➢ ask mentor teacher to complete the first-trimester evaluation by the end of the fifth week.

Hints:

Ask mentor teachers to "think aloud" and explain the "how and why" of their practice. It is important for student teachers to understand the mentor's reasons for managing and instructing the classroom.

Take the initiative and ask for specific feedback. For example, instead of "How am I doing?", ask, "How can I keep the kids focused on instruction during group work?" When student teachers ask specific questions, they are more likely to receive explicit and helpful guidance. After asking for specific feedback, write down the mentor's suggestions and implement the suggestions as soon as possible.

Take a few minutes each day to reflect; What went well? Why did it proceed smoothly? Student teachers should also consider what they would change or modify. Consistent, thoughtful self-analysis helps student teachers improve their lesson planning and delivery.

Develop or update your professional resume. Identify colleagues who are willing to observe lessons and write letters of recommendation.

*****Call or email the University Supervisor with any concerns or questions.*****

➢ continue teaching responsibilities, including classroom organization, lesson planning, instructional delivery, student management, student assessment, parental communication, etc.,

➢ maintain notebook, lesson plans, weekly reflection entries, online discussions, and timecard,

➢ attend seminars and schedule supervisor's observations,

➢ attend district in-service training and parent/teacher conferences,

➢ continue to receive Weekly Progress Forms completed by the mentor, and

➢ ask mentor teacher to complete the second-trimester evaluation by the end of the tenth week.

Hints:

Student teachers should arrange to be videotaped no later than week thirteen. Observe the video (privately, if desired). Initially, self-critique may feel awkward but it is a powerful tool for improving teaching skills. Then identify areas of strength and focus on one area to improve.

The middle five weeks of student teaching are often the most stressful. Take time to eat, rest whenever possible, limit personal commitments and call your university supervisor to discuss concerns and questions. Another way to manage stress is to learn time-saving techniques. Ask a number of veteran teachers for their best time-saving tips regarding grading papers, constructing bulletin boards, developing lesson plans, completing report cards, managing assessment portfolios, etc.

*****Call or e-mail the University Supervisor with any concerns or questions.*****

Phase III – Sustaining Full Responsibility to Phasing Out

> ➢ continue full-time teaching, but gradually phase out during the last two weeks of the student teaching apprenticeship,

> ➢ arrange to videotape yourself teaching a lesson,

> ➢ attend district in-service training, parent/teacher conferences,

> ➢ attend seminars and schedule supervisor's final observations,

> ➢ continue to maintain notebook, lesson plans, weekly reflection entries, online discussions, and timecard,

> ➢ continue to receive Weekly Progress Forms completed by the mentor,

> ➢ arrange to visit other teachers. These observations allow student teachers an opportunity to see exciting and unique classroom practices. Watch management techniques, instructional strategies, and organization of the classroom setting. Take a camera to record bulletin board and/or learning center ideas after receiving permission from the classroom teachers, and

> ➢ complete a professional portfolio. Ask the principal if he/she is willing to conduct a screening interview. (Ask the mentor if this is an appropriate request.)

Hints:

Obtain and complete district job applications, and develop a philosophy of education. Begin to refine your teaching portfolio and collect letters of recommendation.

The end of student teaching is approaching quickly. Remember to stay focused, complete assignments, and develop creative lessons. It is important to clearly decide how and when to phase out. Both the student teacher and mentor need to agree to a phasing-out time line as this avoids confusion and potential frustration. Call the supervisor, if necessary.

Student teachers are encouraged to observe teachers in other schools and in different districts. Student teachers may ask their mentor teacher to offer names of teachers to observe. Most mentors have a network of professional colleagues whom they could recommend. Due to the nature of their job responsibilities, university supervisors have a wide range of contacts, also. Call the teacher at least a week prior to the time of the proposed visit, explain the purpose of the call, and then, if the teacher is agreeable, make an appointment to observe. On the day of the visit, dress professionally, be on time, and be prepared to observe carefully. After the visit, write a thank you note.

During the *last week* of the apprenticeship, the student teacher should

➤ write a thank you note to the mentor teacher, principal, school secretary, and any other professionals who contributed to the student teaching experience,

➤ secure final evaluation. Make several copies and ask mentor and supervisor to sign each copy,

➤ complete timecard in ink and secure signatures (make a copy for your records.),

➤ complete University Supervisor Evaluation (see the Forms section of this text.) (make a copy for your records.), and

➤ turn in all final paperwork at the Certification Event.

Congratulations and welcome to the teaching profession!

NOTES

Chapter 6

Working in an Instructional Team

In many special education settings, student teachers will work not only with a mentor teacher but also with paraprofessionals (sometimes called teacher aides). Part of being a successful special educator depends on the teacher's ability to foster a team relationship among these individuals. Some of the following ideas may help teachers and paraprofessionals build a successful child-centered team.

- Schedule time to plan together. Initially these meetings will focus on learning to work together with the student(s).

- Attend professional development seminars together. This shared activity helps the team member develop common experiences and instructional goals.
- Rotate different responsibilities for supporting all the students in the class. For instance, the teacher and paraprofessional may occasionally switch small groups providing a chance to implement new strategies and measure student growth.
- Engage in exercises, such as the Work Style Survey on the following pages, to develop an awareness of team members working styles and personal needs.

Remember, building and maintaining a successful instructional team takes time and is also a developmental process. It helps to clarify the roles and responsibilities of each team member at the beginning of the year. The following lists typical roles and responsibilities for para-professionals

Classroom Organization and Preparation
- ❑ Assist teacher to maintain records, folders, and filing
- ❑ Manage classroom books, supplies, and equipment
- ❑ Reinforce positive behavior using the classroom management plan
- ❑ Make materials and prepare duplicate materials
- ❑ Report attendance
- ❑ Prepare instructional resources and collect specific materials for lessons
- ❑ Make posters or other visual materials
- ❑ Arrange learning centers and prepare materials for special activities such as art

Instruction
- ❏ Assist in large group instruction
- ❏ Work with individual and small groups of children
- ❏ Help pupils understand teacher directions
- ❏ Collect data for pupil assessment, observe and record behavior
- ❏ Listen and talk with individual students
- ❏ Help pupils improve their social behavior
- ❏ Play instructional games with children
- ❏ Attend student conferences and IEP staffing meetings
- ❏ Listen to oral reading
- ❏ Direct students in use of program materials
- ❏ Contribute ideas when staff is planning instructional program
- ❏ Reteach with special practice after initial instruction by teacher

Supervision
- ❏ Supervise children during recess on the playground
- ❏ Help load bus; walk children to parent pickup area
- ❏ Collect homework and workbooks
- ❏ Help pupils with missed work and makeup tests

While it is clear that paraprofessionals have major responsibilities in the classroom, there are some responsibilities that are **inappropriate** for them to assume.

- ❏ Assign final grades
- ❏ Make retention or promotion decisions
- ❏ Initiate formal contact with parents concerning child's overall progress
- ❏ Administer, score and interpret assessments that require subjective judgment
- ❏ Assume full responsibility for a class for an indefinite amount of time
- ❏ Make major decisions as to the subject matter to be taught
- ❏ Sub for a teacher, unless they are an official substitute in superintendent's office
- ❏ Plan individual daily lesson plans for the classroom
- ❏ Supervise student teachers

Did you know....
Paraprofessionals make up one of the fastest-growing positions in public schools today? In fact, in the early 1960's there were approximately 10,000 paraprofessionals working in public schools, while current estimates range from 300,000 to 500,000. Along with this significant increase in numbers of paraprofessionals in schools, their roles and responsibilities have also expanded significantly. Instead of performing tasks that are primarily noninstructional in nature, paraprofessionals are now involved in activities that are more instructional, such as implementing instruction designed by a certified teacher.

Work Style Survey – Mentor Teacher

Directions: Each member of the teaching team should circle the number that indicates the level of agreement/disagreement with each statement. The teaching team should then compare their responses. In areas where there are significant differences (for example, their response to giving feedback) they should discuss what would be an appropriate compromise. Hopefully this proactive approach to working together will help improve communication and expectations.

Disagree(1) Agree(5)	**I like:**
1　2　3　4　5	1. to supervise others closely
1　2　3　4　5	2. a flexible work schedule
1　2　3　4　5	3. to let team members know exactly what is expected
1　2　3　4　5	4. to provide the materials that will be used
1　2　3　4　5	5. to have a written work schedule
1　2　3　4　5	6. time to think ahead to the next task
1　2　3　4　5	7. to determine instructional methods that will be used
1　2　3　4　5	8. to try new activities independently
1　2　3　4　5	9. to give explicit directions for each task
1　2　3　4　5	10. to do several things at one time
1　2　3　4　5	11. a team that takes on challenges and new situations
1　2　3　4　5	12. taking care of details
1　2　3　4　5	13. to be very punctual
1　2　3　4　5	14. to get frequent feedback on how I can improve
1　2　3　4　5	15. to bring problems out in the open
1　2　3　4　5	16. to give frequent performance feedback
1　2　3　4　5	17. working with other adults
1　2　3　4　5	18. to work alone with little immediate interaction
1　2　3　4　5	19. a quiet place to work without distractions
1　2　3　4　5	20. to work from a written plan

In what areas do we all agree closely?

In what areas do we have large differences?

What steps might be taken to make sure our differences are not creating challenges in the classroom?

Work Style Survey – Student Teacher

Directions: Each member of the teaching team should circle the number that indicates the level of agreement/disagreement with each statement. The teaching team members should then compare their responses. In areas where there are significant differences (for example, their response to giving feedback) they should discuss what would be an appropriate compromise. Hopefully this proactive approach to working together will help improve communication and expectations.

Disagree(1) Agree(5)	I like:
1 2 3 4 5	1. to be supervised closely
1 2 3 4 5	2. a flexible work schedule
1 2 3 4 5	3. to let team members know exactly what is expected
1 2 3 4 5	4. to provide the materials that will be used
1 2 3 4 5	5. to have a written work schedule
1 2 3 4 5	6. time to think ahead to the next task
1 2 3 4 5	7. to determine instructional methods that will be used
1 2 3 4 5	8. to try new activities independently
1 2 3 4 5	9. to give explicit directions for each task
1 2 3 4 5	10. to do several things at one time
1 2 3 4 5	11. a team that takes on challenges and new situations
1 2 3 4 5	12. taking care of details
1 2 3 4 5	13. to be very punctual
1 2 3 4 5	14. to get frequent feedback on how I can improve
1 2 3 4 5	15. to bring problems out in the open
1 2 3 4 5	16. to get frequent performance feedback
1 2 3 4 5	17. working with other adults
1 2 3 4 5	18. to work alone with little immediate interaction
1 2 3 4 5	19. a quiet place to work without distractions
1 2 3 4 5	20. to work from a written plan

In what areas do we all agree closely?

In what areas do we have large differences?

What steps might be taken to make sure our differences are not creating challenges in the classroom?

Work Style Survey – Paraprofessional
Directions: Each member of the teaching team should circle the number that indicates the level of agreement/disagreement with each statement. The teaching team members should then compare their responses. In areas where there are significant differences (for example, their response to giving feedback) they should discuss what would be an appropriate compromise. Hopefully this proactive approach to working together will help improve communication and expectations.

Disagree(1) Agree(5)	I like:
1 2 3 4 5	1. to be supervised closely
1 2 3 4 5	2. a flexible work schedule
1 2 3 4 5	3. to let team members know exactly what is expected
1 2 3 4 5	4. to provide the materials that will be used
1 2 3 4 5	5. to have a written work schedule
1 2 3 4 5	6. time to think ahead to the next task
1 2 3 4 5	7. to determine instructional methods that will be used
1 2 3 4 5	8. to try new activities independently
1 2 3 4 5	9. to give explicit directions for each task
1 2 3 4 5	10. to do several things at one time
1 2 3 4 5	11. a team that takes on challenges and new situations
1 2 3 4 5	12. taking care of details
1 2 3 4 5	13. to be very punctual
1 2 3 4 5	14. to get frequent feedback on how I can improve
1 2 3 4 5	15. to bring problems out in the open
1 2 3 4 5	16. to get frequent performance feedback
1 2 3 4 5	17. working with other adults
1 2 3 4 5	18. to work alone with little immediate interaction
1 2 3 4 5	19. a quiet place to work without distractions
1 2 3 4 5	20. to work from a written plan

In what areas do we all agree closely?

In what areas do we have large differences?

What steps might be taken to make sure our differences are not creating challenges in the classroom?

NOTES

References

- Beeker, R., & Kroeger, M. (1991). *Guidelines for student teaching* (Unpublished Manuscript). Tucson: Teaching and Teacher Education, College of Education, University of Arizona.
- Berliner, D.C. (1982). Recognizing instructional variables. In D. E. Orlosky (Ed.) in *Introduction to education* (pp.198-222). Columbus, OH: Merrill.
- Burgoon, J.K., D.B. Buller and W.G. Woodall (1989). *Nonverbal communications: 1 unspoken dialogue.* New York: Harper and Row.
- Enz, B.J., Carlile, B. (1997) *Seeing the forest…and the trees: Helping student teachers and mentors assess and improve instruction.* Paper Presentation, Association of Teacher Educators, Washington, D.C.
- Enz, B.J., Carlile, B., Freeman, D. & Wrana, J. (1995). *Student teachers and mentor conversations: A study of the nature and impact of instructional feedback.* Paper presentation at the Annual Meeting of the American Education Research Association, San Francisco, CA.
- Enz, B. J., Freeman, D. J., & Wallin, M. (1993). Roles and responsibilities of the student teaching supervisor: Matches and mismatches in perceptions. In D.J. McIntyre and D. M. Byrd (Eds.), *Preparing tomorrow's teachers: The field experience* (pp.131-150). Thousand Oaks, CA: Association of Teacher Education, Corwin Press, Inc.
- Gagne, R.M., Briggs, L.J., & Wager, W.W. (1992). *Principles of instructional design*, (4th   ed.).: Harcourt Brace Jovanovich. Fort Worth, TX.
- Lasley, T. J. (1981). Research perspectives on classroom management. *Journal of Teacher Education*, 32(2), 14-17.

Related Resources

- Berliner, D.C. & Casanova, U. (1993). *Putting research to work in your school.* New York: Scholastic, Inc.
- Bondy, E., Ross, D.; Gallingane, C. Hambacher, E. (2007). Creating environments of success and resilience: Culturally responsive classroom management and more. *Urban Education,* 42(4). 326-348.
- Brophy, J.E. & Evertson, C. M. (1976). *Learning from teaching: A developmental perspective.* Allyn and Bacon. Boston: MA.
- Brophy, J.E., & Good, T.L. (1986). Teacher behavior and student achievement. In M.C. Wittrock (Ed), *Handbook of research on teaching* (3rd ed. pp.328-376). New York: Macmillan.
- Capie, W., Anderson, S.J., Johnson C.E. & Ellett, C.D. (1979). *Teacher performance assessment instruments: A handbook for interpretation.* Athens: Teacher Assessment Project, College of Education, University of Georgia.
- Comber, B. & Nichols, S. (2004). Getting the big picture: Regulating knowledge in the early childhood literacy curriculum. *Journal of Early Childhood Literacy,* 4(1). 43-63.
- Costa, A.L., & Garmston, R.J. (1994). *Cognitive coaching: A foundation for renaissance.* Norwood, MA: Christopher-Gordon Publishers, Inc.
- Daresh, J. C. & Playko, M.A. (1995). *Supervision as a proactive process: Concepts and cases* (2nd Ed.) Prospect Heights, IL: Waveland Press, Inc.
- Doyle, W. (1978). Paradigms for research on teaching effectiveness. In L.S. Shulman (Ed.), *Review of research in education* (Vol. 5, pp. 163-198). Itasca, IL: F. E. Peacock.
- Duffy, G.G. & Roehler, L.R. (1986). *Improving reading instruction through the use of responsive elaboration.* East Lansing: Institute for Research on Teaching, Michigan State University.
- Eby, J. W. (1996). *Reflective planning, teaching and evaluation, K-12* (2nd Ed.) Columbus, OH: Merrill
- Enz, B.J., Anderson, G.W., Weber, B.J. & Lawhead, D. (1992). The Arizona teacher residency program: Commitment, collaboration, and collegiality. In G. Debolt (Ed.), *Teacher induction and mentoring: School-based collaborative programs.* Albany, NY: SUNY Press.
- Evertson, C. & Weinstein, C.S.(2006), *Handbook of classroom management: Research, practice, and contemporary issues.* Lawrence Erlbaum Associates Philadelphia, PA
- Fisher, C.W., Filby, N.V., Marliave, R., Cahen, L.S., Dishaw, M.M., Moore, J.E., & Berliner, D.C. (1978). *Beginning teacher evaluation study* (Technical Report, V-1). San Francisco: Far West Laboratory.
- French, L. (2004). Science as the center of a coherent, integrated early childhood curriculum. *Early Childhood Research Quarterly,* 19(1). 138-149.
- Gage, N.L. & Berliner, D.C. (1984). *Educational psychology* (3rd Ed.) Boston: Houghton Mifflin.
- Gagne, E. (1985). Strategies for effective teaching and learning. *The cognitive psychology of school learning.* Boston: Little, Brown.

- Gick, R. (1993). *Student teacher's guidelines*. Tempe: AZ. College of Education, Arizona State University.
- Glatthorn, A. (1995). Teacher development in L.W. Andersen (Ed.) *International encyclopedia of teaching and teacher education*, (2nd Ed. pp.41-46). Elsevier Science Ltd., Cambridge University Press.
- Honig, A. Miller, S, & Church, E. (2006). Helping children feel comfortable and calm. *Early Childhood Today*, 21(1). 27-33.
- Horn, P.J. (1989, July) *Teacher empowerment begins with the College of Education*. Paper Presentation for the Association of Independent Liberal Arts Colleges, Indianapolis, IN.
- Hunter, M. (1982). *Mastery teaching*. El Segundo, CA: TIP Publications.
- Levin, T. & Lang, R. (1981). *Effective instruction*. Alexandria, VA: Association for Supervision and Curriculum Development.
- Li, Y. L. (2006). Classroom organization: Understanding the context in which children are expected to learn. *Early Childhood Education Journal*, 34(1). 37-43.
- Lobman, C. L. (2006). Improvisation: An analytic tool for examining teacher-child interactions in the early childhood classroom. *Early Childhood Research Quarterly*, 21(4). 455-470.
- Lybolt, J., Armstrong, J. Evans, K., & Gottfred, C. (2007). *Building language throughout the year: The preschool early literacy curriculum*. Brookes Publishing Company. Baltimore, MD.
- Morrow, L.M. (2007). *Developing literacy in preschool: Tools for teaching literacy*. Guilford Publications, New York: NY.
- Moyles, J. (2006). *Effective leadership and management in the early years*. Open University Press. New York: NY.
- Olness, R. (2007). *Using literature to enhance content area instruction: A guide for K-5 teachers*. International Reading Association. Reston, VA.
- Pitten, D.E. (1998). *Stories of student teaching: A case approach to the student teachingexperience*. Columbus, OH: Merrill.
- Roe, B.D. & Ross, E.P. (1994). *Student teaching and field experiences handbook*. (4th Ed.) Columbus, OH: Merrill.
- Rosenshine, B.V. & Meyer, L. (1978). Staff development for teaching basic skills. *Theory into practice*, 27, 267-271.
- Rosenshine, B.V. & Stevens, R. (1986). Teacher Functions. In M.C. Wittrock (Ed.) *Handbook of research on teaching* (pp.376-391). New York: Macmillan.
- Saloman, G. (1992). The changing role of the teacher: From information transmitter to orchestrator of learning. In F.K. Oser, A. Dick & J. L. Patry (Eds.), *Effective and responsible teaching: The new synthesis* (pp. 35-49). San Francisco: Jossey-Bass, Inc.
- Schon, D.A. (1983). *The reflective practitioner: How professionals think in action*. New York: Basic books.
- Shavelson, R.J. (1983). Review of research on teachers' pedagogical judgements, plans and decisions. *Elementary School Journal, 83*, 392-413.
- Shavelson, R.J. 8 Borko, H. (1979). Research on teachers' decisions in planning instruction. *Educational Horizons*, 57, 183-189.

- Stallings, J.A. & Kasbowckz, D. (1974). *Follow through classroom observation evaluation, 1972-73*. Menlo Park, CA: Stanford Research Institute.
- Stiggins, R.J. (1986, April). *Lessons from the observations of classroom assessment environments.* Paper Presentation at the Annual Meeting of the American Educational Research Association, San Francisco, CA.
- Terpstra, J.E., & Tamura, R. (2008). Effective sociat interaction strategies for inclusive settings. *Early Childhood Education Journal*, 35(5). 405-411.
- Warner, C., Hartgraves, J., Ryan, R., Reno, T.R. & Brunstein, J. J. (1983). *Arizona teacher residency project instrument*. Phoenix: Arizona Department of Education.

- Wilburne, J. Napoli, M. Keat, J.B., Dile, K. Trout, M., & Decker, S. (2007). Journeying into mathematics through storybooks: A kindergarten story. *Teaching Children Mathematics,* 14(4). 232-237.

Week # ________________________   Date ________________________

WEEKLY PROGRESS FORM

The Weekly Progress Form has been designed to help mentor and student teacher teams give and receive frequent feedback. After checking the items on each instrument, Please write comments that provide specific guidance to the student teacher.

Professional Attributes and Characteristics Scale

1. Attendance
- ☐ Frequently absent
- ☐ Rarely absent
- ☐ Exemplary Attendance

2. Punctuality
- ☐ Frequently late
- ☐ Generally punctual
- ☐ Always on time

3. Professional Appearance
- ☐ Occasionally appears inappropriately/ unprofessionally dressed
- ☐ Is usually dressed appropriately
- ☐ Always dresses/appears in a professional manner

4. Oral Expression
- ☐ Makes frequent usage and/or grammatical errors
- ☐ Inarticulate
- ☐ Articulate
- ☐ Expressive, animated

5. Written Expression
- ☐ Written work contains misspellings, and/or grammatical errors
- ☐ Writing is often unclear and disorganized
- ☐ Written work is organized and clearly expresses ideas
- ☐ Uses written forms to effectively communicate with parents, administrators, and/or colleagues

6. Tact, Judgment
- ☐ Thoughtless: insensitive to other's feelings and opinions
- ☐ Somewhat or sometimes insensitive and undiplomatic
- ☐ Perceives what to do or say in order to maintain good relations with others and responds accordingly
- ☐ Diplomatic: highly sensitive to other's feelings and opinions

7. Reliability/Dependability
- ☐ Sometimes fails to complete assigned tasks and duties
- ☐ Sometimes needs to be reminded to attend to assigned tasks and duties
- ☐ Responsible: attends to assigned tasks and duties on schedule without prompting
- ☐ Self-starter: perceives needs and attends to them immediately

8. Self-Initiative/Independence
- ☐ Passive: depends on others for direction, ideas and guidance
- ☐ Has good ideas, works effectively with limited supervision
- ☐ Creative and resourceful, independently implements plans

9. Self-Confidence
- ☐ Anxious: often appears self-conscious, nervous
- ☐ Arrogant: has unfounded belief in abilities
- ☐ Usually confident – comfortable in classroom situations
- ☐ Realistically self-assured: competently handles class demands

10. Collegiality
- ☐ Prefers to work in isolation
- ☐ Reluctant to share ideas and materials
- ☐ Often participates in team efforts
- ☐ Willingly shares ideas and materials

11. Interaction with Students
- ☐ Can appear threatening or antagonistic towards students
- ☐ Shy: hesitant to work with students
- ☐ Relates easily and positively with students
- ☐ Outgoing: actively seeks opportunities to work with students

12. Response to Students' Needs
- ☐ Does not attempt to accommodate needs of unique learners
- ☐ Makes negative comments about students' abilities to learn
- ☐ Usually accepts responsibility for all students' learning
- ☐ Consistently responds to learning needs of all students

13. Response to Feedback
- ☐ Defensive – unreceptive to feedback
- ☐ Receptive – but doesn't implement suggestions
- ☐ Receptive – and adjusts performance accordingly
- ☐ Eager - Solicits suggestions and feedback from others

14. Ability to Reflect and Improve Performance
- ☐ Reluctant to analyze teaching performance
- ☐ Makes some effort to review teaching skills
- ☐ Actively seeks ways to assess teaching abilities
- ☐ Consistently deepens knowledge of classroom practice and students' learning

15. Professional Characteristics   S=Seldom,   U = Usually,   A=Always

S U A   The Student Teacher:

- ☐☐☐ **Commitment** – demonstrates genuine concern for students and is dedicated to the teaching profession
- ☐☐☐ **Creativity** – seeks opportunities to provide unique learning experiences and develops imaginative lessons
- ☐☐☐ **Flexibility** – responds to unforeseen circumstances in appropriate manner and modifies actions or plans when necessary
- ☐☐☐ **Integrity** – maintains high ethical and professional standards and responds to district policies appropriately
- ☐☐☐ **Organization** – is efficient; successfully manages multiple tasks simultaneously and establishes/maintains effective classroom routines/procedures
- ☐☐☐ **Perseverance** – strives to complete tasks and improve teaching skills
- ☐☐☐ **Positive Disposition** – possesses pleasant interpersonal skills, is patient, resilient, optimistic and approachable

Identify two areas of instructional strength your student teacher demonstrated this week (Indicate with a "+"). Then identify one area that the student teacher needs to focus on the next week (Indicate with a "✓").
See the *Coaching the Special Education Student Teacher (Dual Certification)* for coaching suggestions (correlating pages indicated)

Instructional Development Scale	Area	
	Designs and Plans Instruction	**Pages 77-103**
	1. Specifies desired learner outcomes for lessons	
	2. Specifies teaching procedures for lessons	
	3. Specifies resources for lessons	
	4. Specifies procedures for assessing student progress	
	5. Plans for student diversity, abilities and styles	
	6. Plans address all levels of knowledge and understanding	
	Creates and Maintains a Learning Climate	**Pages 104-118**
	7. Communicates enthusiasm for student learning	
	8. Demonstrates warmth and friendliness	
	9. Shows sensitivity to needs/feelings of students	
	10. Provides feedback to students about behavior	
	11. Maintains positive classroom behavior	
	12. Manages disruptive behavior	

Area	
Implements and Manages Instruction and Assessment	**Pages 119-147**
13. Begins lesson effectively	
14. Presents information clearly	
15. Gives clear directions and explanations	
16. Uses student responses/questions in teaching	
17. Maximizes opportunities for all to participate	
18. Provides students feedback throughout lesson	
19. Promotes student retention and understanding	
20. Uses effective closure/summarization techniques	
21. Uses instructional material effectively	
22. Promotes individual student learning	
23. Uses teaching methods appropriately/effectively	
24. Uses instructional time effectively	
25. Demonstrates knowledge of subject	
26. Manages conditions for teaching and learning	

If there are attributes or instructional competencies that need more attention, please provide explicit examples of how student teacher may strengthen this area. For example: **Area of Concern: Pacing**	
Vague suggestions:	**Explicit written directions:**
Your lesson ran long, remember, pacing is important, so keep it moving.	Have your material ready. Outline your procedures. Make a timeline and keep the clock in sight.

____
Student Teacher Signature

____
Mentor Teacher Signature

GUIDE FOR THE PROFESSIONAL ATTRIBUTES AND CHARACTERISTICS
AND
INSTRUCTIONAL DEVELOPMENT SCALES

Please print or type

Student Teacher________________________________ Date ____________________

ID. # ___________________________ Undergraduate ☐   Graduate ☐

School Name ____________________________ District________________________

Student Teacher ________________________________ Date ____________________
Signature

Mentor Teacher *(Print Name)* ____

Mentor Teacher ________________________________ Date ____________________
Signature

University Supervisor *(Print Name)* ________________________________

University Supervisor ________________________________ Date ______________
Signature

Directions

The purpose of the Professional Attributes and Characteristics & Instructional Development Scales is to provide the Office of Professional Field Experiences with specific, pertinent information regarding the student teacher's progress and is designed to assess beginning teacher performance in two areas.

THE PROFESSIONAL ATTRIBUTES AND CHARACTERISTICS SCALE consists of 16 items. For each attribute, please place a check mark before the one adjective or statement that describes the behavior the student teacher typically displays. Please elaborate further in the comments section when additional feedback will help the student teacher continue to progress.

THE INSTRUCTIONAL DEVELOPMENT SCALE consists of 26 discrete items in three subsections: Designs and Plans Instruction, Creates and Maintains a Learning Climate, Implements and Manages Instruction and Assessment. For each item, please place a check mark before all the descriptors that have been actually observed. Please elaborate further in the comment section when additional feedback will help the student continue to progress. Next, choose a level of overall proficiency for the item by bubbling in the appropriate number above the descriptors.

Example:

12) Manages Disruptive Behavior	Proficiency Levels
① ② ❸ ④ ⑤	① ② ❸ ④ ⑤
☐ Individuals who have caused disruptions are dealt with rather than the entire class being punished. ☑ Major disruptions are attended to quickly and appropriately. ☑ Consequences for misbehavior are based on the severity of the disruption. ☐ Disruptive behavior rarely occurs. Comments:	**Level 1** Student teacher has not yet developed or used this skill. **Level 2** Student teacher is beginning to incorporate this skill. **Level 3** Student teaches uses this skill appropriately. **Level 4** Student teacher uses this skill appropriately and consistently. **Level 5** Student teacher uses this skill appropriately and consistently, with a high degree of competence and confidence.

PROFESSIONAL ATTRIBUTES AND CHARACTERISTICS SCALE

1) Attendance

☐ Frequently absent
☐ Rarely absent
☐ Exemplary attendance

2) Punctuality

☐ Frequently late
☐ Generally punctual
☐ Always on time

3) Professional Appearance

☐ Occasionally appears inappropriately/unprofessionally dressed
☐ Is usually dressed appropriately
☐ Always dresses/appears in a professional manner

4) Oral Expression

☐ Makes frequent usage and/or grammatical errors
☐ Inarticulate
☐ Articulate
☐ Expressive, animated

5) Written Expression

☐ Written work contains misspellings and/or grammatical errors
☐ Written work is often unclear and disorganized
☐ Written work is organized and clearly expresses ideas

6) Tact/judgment

☐ Thoughtless: highly insensitive to others' feelings and opinions
☐ Somewhat or sometimes insensitive and undiplomatic
☐ Perceives what to do or say in order to maintain good relations with others and responds accordingly
☐ Diplomatic: highly sensitive to others' feelings and opinions

7) Reliability/Dependability

☐ Sometimes fails to complete assigned tasks and duties
☐ Sometimes needs to be reminded to attend to assigned tasks/duties
☐ Responsible: attends to assigned tasks/duties on schedule without prompting
☐ Self-starter: perceives needs and attends to them immediately

8) Self-Initiative/Independence

☐ Passive: depends on others for directions, ideas and guidance
☐ Has good ideas, works effectively with limited supervision
☐ Creative and resourceful: independently implements plans

9) Self-confidence

☐ Anxious: often appears self-conscious, nervous
☐ Arrogant: has unfounded belief in abilities
☐ Usually confident – comfortable in classroom situations
☐ Realistically self-assured: competently handles class demands

10) Collegiality

☐ Often works in isolation
☐ Reluctant to share ideas and materials
☐ Willingly shares ideas and materials

11) Interaction with Students

☐ Can appear threatening or antagonistic towards students
☐ Shy: hesitant to work with students
☐ Relates easily and positively with students
☐ Outgoing: actively seeks opportunities to work with students

12) Response to Students' Needs

☐ Does not attempt to accommodate needs of unique learners
☐ Makes negative comments about students' ability to learn
☐ Usually accepts responsibility for all students' learning
☐ Consistently responds to the learning needs of all students

<table>
<tr><td>STUDENT TEACHER NAME</td><td>ID #</td><td>DATE</td></tr>
</table>

13) Response to feedback

☐ Defensive: unreceptive to feedback
☐ Receptive: but doesn't implement suggestions
☐ Receptive: and adjusts performance accordingly
☐ Eager: solicits suggestions and feedback from others

14) Ability to Reflect and Improve Performance

☐ Reluctant to analyze performance
☐ Makes some effort to review skills
☐ Actively seeks ways to assess abilities
☐ Consistently deepens knowledge of classroom practice and student learning

15) Professional Characteristics

Seldom	Usually	Always	
			For each characteristic check the frequency indicator that most accurately reflects the student teacher behavior.
☐	☐	☐	<u>Commitment</u> – Demonstrates genuine concern for students and is dedicated to the teaching profession
☐	☐	☐	<u>Creativity</u> – seeks opportunities to develop imaginative instructional lessons
☐	☐	☐	<u>Flexibility</u> – responds to unforeseen circumstances in appropriate manner and modifies actions or plans when necessary
☐	☐	☐	<u>Integrity</u> – maintains high ethical and professional standards
☐	☐	☐	<u>Organization</u> – is efficient, successfully manages multiple tasks simultaneously
☐	☐	☐	<u>Perseverance</u> – strives to complete tasks and improve teaching skills
☐	☐	☐	<u>Positive Disposition</u> – possesses pleasant interpersonal skills: is patient, resilient, optimistic, approachable

16) Potential as a Teacher

☐ Recommend review of career options and consideration of profession other than teaching
☐ Recommend continuation in teaching profession
☐ Highly recommend continuation in teaching profession: strong candidate

Comments:

<table>
<tr><td>STUDENT TEACHER NAME</td><td>ID #</td><td>DATE</td></tr>
<tr><td></td><td></td><td></td></tr>
</table>

INSTRUCTIONAL DEVELOPMENT SCALE

The Instructional Development Scale consists of 26 discrete items in three subsections: Designs and Plans Instruction, Creates and Maintains a Learning Climate, Implements and Manages Instruction and Assessment.

Directions:

    a) For each scale please mark only the descriptors that were actually observed.

    b) Next, choose a level of overall proficiency for each scale.

    Level ① = Student teacher has not yet developed or used this skill.

    Level ② = Student teacher is beginning to incorporate this skill.

    Level ③ = Student teacher uses this skill appropriately.

    Level ④ = Student teacher uses this skill appropriately and consistently.

    Level ⑤ = Student teacher uses this skill appropriately and consistently, with a high degree of competence and confidence.

Note: Proficiency level does not necessarily correspond to the number of check marks given.

Designs and Plans Instruction

1) Specifies desired learner outcomes for lessons ① ② ③ ④ ⑤	**2) Specifies teaching procedures for lessons** ① ② ③ ④ ⑤	**3) Specifies resources for lessons** ① ② ③ ④ ⑤
☐ Desired learner outcome(s) described in clear and consistent terms. ☐ Logically sequenced. ☐ Appropriate to student achievement level(s). ☐ Directly linked to unit goals and to state/district/school standards.	☐ Referenced to the objective(s)/outcome(s). ☐ Appropriate to accomplishing objective(s)/outcome(s). ☐ Logically sequenced. ☐ Transitions are planned from one activity to another.	☐ Relevance to learning activity. ☐ Lesson plans include specific description of resources, such as title, page, equipment. ☐ Concrete or manipulative materials are identified when appropriate. ☐ Creative use of resources.
Comments:	Comments:	Comments:
4) Specifies procedures for assessing student progress ① ② ③ ④ ⑤	**5) Plans for student diversity, abilities and styles** ① ② ③ ④ ⑤	**6) Plans address all levels of knowledge and understanding** ① ② ③ ④ ⑤
☐ Written lesson plans include informal assessments of student learning. ☐ Tests and other formal assessments focus directly on instructional goals and objectives and assess only the content that was taught. ☐ Develops and maintains an accurate record of student performance, e.g. grade book, anecdotal notes, test scores, portfolio. ☐ Considers multiple sources of assessment data when making instructional decisions.	☐ Presents instruction based on assessment of student's performance. ☐ Provides remedial or enrichment materials/instruction when appropriate. ☐ Plans individual student conferences to discuss learning or motivational problems. ☐ Varies instructional strategies in accordance with student needs.	☐ Plans require students to memorize important vs. trivial information and to comprehend or interpret information as appropriate. ☐ Plans require students to apply information to real life settings. ☐ Plans require students to identify/clarify complex ideas or to synthesize knowledge by integrating information. ☐ Plans stress depth as well as breadth of content coverage.
Comments:	Comments:	Comments:

<table>
<tr><td>STUDENT TEACHER NAME</td><td>ID #</td><td>DATE</td></tr>
</table>

Creates and Maintains a Learning Climate

7) Communicates enthusiasm for student learning ① ② ③ ④ ⑤	**8) Demonstrates warmth and friendliness** ① ② ③ ④ ⑤	**9) Shows sensitivity to needs and feelings of students** ① ② ③ ④ ⑤
☐ Eye contact or facial expressions communicate pleasure, concern, interest, etc. ☐ Voice inflections stress points of interest and importance. ☐ Communicates enthusiasm through movement in the classroom. ☐ Gestures accentuate points.	☐ Asks about student's interests and opinions. ☐ Interacts in a relaxed and informal way with students. ☐ Moves freely among students. ☐ Uses students' names in a warm and friendly way.	☐ Students are reinforced when they do well. ☐ Students are encouraged when they have difficulty. ☐ Students' contributions are accepted in a positive manner. ☐ Students are treated with respect and courtesy.
Comments:	Comments:	Comments:
10) Provides feedback to students about behavior ① ② ③ ④ ⑤	**11) Maintains positive classroom behavior** ① ② ③ ④ ⑤	**12) Manages disruptive behavior** ① ② ③ ④ ⑤
☐ Student teacher clearly states expectations about appropriate behavior. ☐ Student teacher provides verbal feedback for acceptable behavior. ☐ Student teacher provides non-verbal feedback for acceptable or unacceptable behavior. ☐ Student teacher's language is free of derogatory references or sarcasm.	☐ Techniques that help students learn self-management and personal responsibility are utilized. ☐ Inconsequential behavior problems are overlooked or none exist. ☐ Appropriate behavior is reinforced. ☐ Appropriate student behaviors are maintained by maximizing opportunities for each individual to succeed.	☐ Individuals who have caused disruptions are dealt with rather than entire class being punished. ☐ Major disruptions are attended to quickly and appropriately. ☐ Consequences for misbehavior are based on the severity of the disruption. ☐ Disruptive behavior rarely occurs.
Comments:	Comments:	Comments:

<table>
<tr><td>STUDENT TEACHER NAME</td><td>ID #</td><td>DATE</td></tr>
</table>

Implements and Manages Instruction and Assessment

13) Begins lesson effectively

① ② ③ ④ ⑤

- ☐ Student teacher activates/establishes students' prior knowledge of current lesson.
- ☐ Student teacher helps students to understand the purpose or importance of the lesson.
- ☐ Student teacher links new information to students' existing knowledge.
- ☐ Student teacher stimulates interest in lesson by actively involving students or by asking thought-provoking questions.

Comments:

14) Presents information clearly

① ② ③ ④ ⑤

- ☐ Student teacher directly relates information to desired learner outcomes.
- ☐ Student teacher presents information in a logical sequence.
- ☐ Student teacher provides concrete and/or visual models when appropriate.
- ☐ Student teacher uses vocabulary appropriate to students' level of understanding.

Comments:

15) Gives clear directions and explanations

① ② ③ ④ ⑤

- ☐ Student teacher presents directions in a logical sequence.
- ☐ Student teacher writes critical information on board, chart or overhead.
- ☐ Student teacher clearly informs students what they should be doing, where to do it, and for how long.
- ☐ Student teacher checks students' understanding of directions before they practice independently.

Comments:

16) Uses students responses and questions in teaching

① ② ③ ④ ⑤

- ☐ Student teacher encourages students' responses and/or questions.
- ☐ Student teacher responds in a positive and supportive manner.
- ☐ Student teacher incorporates student responses and questions into the lesson.
- ☐ Student teacher uses responses to monitor student understanding of the information presented.

Comments:

17) Maximizes opportunities for all to participate

① ② ③ ④ ⑤

- ☐ Student teacher asks questions of whole group first, rather than individuals.
- ☐ Student teacher provides ample wait-time for all students after asking questions and redirects accordingly.
- ☐ Student teacher offers frequent opportunities for student-to-student interactions/inquiry.
- ☐ Student teacher provides many opportunities for covert/overt participation; physical movement, small group activities, discussions.

Comments:

18) Provides students feedback throughout lesson

① ② ③ ④ ⑤

- ☐ Student teacher provides feedback to students as soon as possible.
- ☐ Student teacher provides feedback to students in a positive manner.
- ☐ Student teacher reviews students' strengths and weaknesses and offers suggestions on how performance can be improved.
- ☐ Student teacher helps students evaluate their own performance.

Comments:

19) Promotes student retention and understanding

① ② ③ ④ ⑤

- ☐ Student teacher uses techniques which help make material relevant to students and explains the importance of the lesson.
- ☐ Student teacher defines or models the expectations of the lesson or learning.
- ☐ Student teacher provides opportunity for all students to demonstrate an understanding of what is being taught.
- ☐ Student teacher monitors student responses, interprets the source of student errors, and adjusts instruction accordingly.

Comments:

20) Uses effective closure or summarization technique

① ② ③ ④ ⑤

- ☐ Student teacher gives students an opportunity for closure/ summarization at the end of distinct segments within the lesson or between objectives.
- ☐ Student teacher provides opportunity for the student to summarize at the end of each lesson.
- ☐ Student teacher actively involves students in their own closure/summarization.
- ☐ Student teacher extends closure/summarization to future applications or actions.

Comments:

21) Uses instructional material effectively

① ② ③ ④ ⑤

- ☐ Student teacher uses instructional equipment and other aids, such as charts, graphs, overhead, video, slides, software, maps and/or manipulatives.
- ☐ Student teacher uses instructional resources that contribute to the students' understanding of lesson goals/objectives.
- ☐ Student teacher smoothly blends media with other types of instruction.
- ☐ Student teacher creates original instructional aids which are relevant and enhance the effectiveness of the teaching.

Comments:

22) Promotes individual student learning

① ② ③ ④ ⑤

- ☐ Materials chosen are directly related to the goals/objectives of the lesson.
- ☐ Materials selected ensure appropriate level of student success.
- ☐ Students are given ample opportunity to use materials as intended.
- ☐ Students' interaction with the materials is monitored to determine their level of understanding.

Comments:

23) Uses teaching methods appropriately/effectively

① ② ③ ④ ⑤

- ☐ Student teacher uses a variety of methods within the lesson: drill, inquiry, discussion, role playing, demonstration, explanation, problem-solving, cooperative learning.
- ☐ Student teacher uses method(s) that accomplish desired outcome(s).
- ☐ Student teacher adjusts instructional methods according to student progress.
- ☐ Student teacher makes smooth transitions between instructional activities within a lesson.

Comments:

24) Uses instructional time effectively

① ② ③ ④ ⑤

- ☐ Activities begin on schedule.
- ☐ Allocated instructional time is maximized.
- ☐ Instructional pacing is appropriate for students.
- ☐ There are no significant delays or periods of time during which the students are not effectively engaged.

Comments:

25) Demonstrates knowledge of subject	**26) Manages conditions for teaching and learning**
① ② ③ ④ ⑤	① ② ③ ④ ⑤
☐ Student teacher's subject area knowledge is accurate and current. ☐ Information and materials present concepts and ideas in multiple ways. ☐ Student teacher asks higher order questions and/or builds on students' questions. ☐ Student teacher is enthusiastic about content area and is able to involve or motivate students in subject matter.	☐ Basic management skills are implemented to efficiently and effectively instruct the class. Instructional tools are readily accessible. ☐ Student interactions are facilitated by room arrangements. ☐ Routine tasks are handled smoothly by teacher and/or students (attendance, lunch count, etc.). ☐ Materials and supplies are readily available. Distribution and collection of materials have been planned.
Comments:	Comments:

GUIDE FOR THE PROFESSIONAL ATTRIBUTES AND CHARACTERISTICS
AND
INSTRUCTIONAL DEVELOPMENT SCALES

Please print or type

Student Teacher_________________________________ Date _________________________

ID. # _________________________________ Undergraduate ☐   Graduate ☐

School Name _________________________________ District_________________________

Student Teacher _________________________________ Date _________________________
  Signature

Mentor Teacher *(Print Name)* ____

Mentor Teacher _________________________________ Date _________________________
  Signature

University Supervisor *(Print Name)* ____

University Supervisor _________________________________ Date _____________________
  Signature

Directions

The purpose of the Professional Attributes and Characteristics & Instructional Development Scales is to provide the Office of Professional Field Experiences with specific, pertinent information regarding the student teacher's progress and is designed to assess beginning teacher performance in two areas.

THE PROFESSIONAL ATTRIBUTES AND CHARACTERISTICS SCALE consists of 16 items. For each attribute, please place a check mark before the one adjective or statement that describes the behavior the student teacher typically displays. Please elaborate further in the comments section when additional feedback will help the student teacher continue to progress.

THE INSTRUCTIONAL DEVELOPMENT SCALE consists of 26 discrete items in three subsections: Designs and Plans Instruction, Creates and Maintains a Learning Climate, Implements and Manages Instruction and Assessment. For each item, please place a check mark before all the descriptors that have been actually observed. Please elaborate further in the comment section when additional feedback will help the student continue to progress. Next, choose a level of overall proficiency for the item by bubbling in the appropriate number above the descriptors.

Example:

<table>
<tr><td>

12) Manages Disruptive Behavior

①   ②   ❸   ④   ⑤

☐ Individuals who have caused disruptions are dealt with rather than the entire class being punished.
☑ Major disruptions are attended to quickly and appropriately.
☑ Consequences for misbehavior are based on the severity of the disruption.
☐ Disruptive behavior rarely occurs.

Comments:

</td><td>

Proficiency Levels

①   ②   ❸   ④   ⑤

Level 1 Student teacher has not yet developed or used this skill.
Level 2 Student teacher is beginning to incorporate this skill.
Level 3 Student teaches uses this skill appropriately.
Level 4 Student teacher uses this skill appropriately and consistently.
Level 5 Student teacher uses this skill appropriately and consistently, with a high degree of competence and confidence.

</td></tr>
</table>

<table><tr><td>STUDENT TEACHER NAME</td><td>ID #</td><td>DATE</td></tr><tr><td></td><td></td><td></td></tr></table>

PROFESSIONAL ATTRIBUTES AND CHARACTERISTICS SCALE

1) Attendance

☐ Frequently absent
☐ Rarely absent
☐ Exemplary attendance

2) Punctuality

☐ Frequently late
☐ Generally punctual
☐ Always on time

3) Professional Appearance

☐ Occasionally appears inappropriately/unprofessionally dressed
☐ Is usually dressed appropriately
☐ Always dresses/appears in a professional manner

4) Oral Expression

☐ Makes frequent usage and/or grammatical errors
☐ Inarticulate
☐ Articulate
☐ Expressive, animated

5) Written Expression

☐ Written work contains misspellings and/or grammatical errors
☐ Written work is often unclear and disorganized
☐ Written work is organized and clearly expresses ideas

6) Tact/judgment

☐ Thoughtless: highly insensitive to others' feelings and opinions
☐ Somewhat or sometimes insensitive and undiplomatic
☐ Perceives what to do or say in order to maintain good relations with others and responds accordingly
☐ Diplomatic: highly sensitive to others' feelings and opinions

7) Reliability/Dependability

☐ Sometimes fails to complete assigned tasks and duties
☐ Sometimes needs to be reminded to attend to assigned tasks/duties
☐ Responsible: attends to assigned tasks/duties on schedule without prompting
☐ Self-starter: perceives needs and attends to them immediately

8) Self-Initiative/Independence

☐ Passive: depends on others for directions, ideas and guidance
☐ Has good ideas, works effectively with limited supervision
☐ Creative and resourceful: independently implements plans

9) Self-confidence

☐ Anxious: often appears self-conscious, nervous
☐ Arrogant: has unfounded belief in abilities
☐ Usually confident – comfortable in classroom situations
☐ Realistically self-assured: competently handles class demands

10) Collegiality

☐ Often works in isolation
☐ Reluctant to share ideas and materials
☐ Willingly shares ideas and materials

11) Interaction with Students

☐ Can appear threatening or antagonistic towards students
☐ Shy: hesitant to work with students
☐ Relates easily and positively with students
☐ Outgoing: actively seeks opportunities to work with students

12) Response to Students' Needs

☐ Does not attempt to accommodate needs of unique learners
☐ Makes negative comments about students' ability to learn
☐ Usually accepts responsibility for all students' learning
☐ Consistently responds to the learning needs of all students

<table>
<tr><td colspan="3">STUDENT TEACHER NAME</td><td>ID #</td><td>DATE</td></tr>
<tr><td colspan="3"></td><td></td><td></td></tr>
</table>

13) Response to feedback

☐ Defensive: unreceptive to feedback
☐ Receptive: but doesn't implement suggestions
☐ Receptive: and adjusts performance accordingly
☐ Eager: solicits suggestions and feedback from others

14) Ability to Reflect and Improve Performance

☐ Reluctant to analyze performance
☐ Makes some effort to review skills
☐ Actively seeks ways to assess abilities
☐ Consistently deepens knowledge of classroom practice and student learning

15) Professional Characteristics

Seldom	Usually	Always	For each characteristic check the frequency indicator that most accurately reflects the student teacher behavior.
☐	☐	☐	<u>Commitment</u> – Demonstrates genuine concern for students and is dedicated to the teaching profession
☐	☐	☐	<u>Creativity</u> – seeks opportunities to develop imaginative instructional lessons
☐	☐	☐	<u>Flexibility</u> – responds to unforeseen circumstances in appropriate manner and modifies actions or plans when necessary
☐	☐	☐	<u>Integrity</u> – maintains high ethical and professional standards
☐	☐	☐	<u>Organization</u> – is efficient, successfully manages multiple tasks simultaneously
☐	☐	☐	<u>Perseverance</u> – strives to complete tasks and improve teaching skills
☐	☐	☐	<u>Positive Disposition</u> – possesses pleasant interpersonal skills: is patient, resilient, optimistic, approachable

16) Potential as a Teacher

☐ Recommend review of career options and consideration of profession other than teaching
☐ Recommend continuation in teaching profession
☐ Highly recommend continuation in teaching profession: strong candidate

Comments:

INSTRUCTIONAL DEVELOPMENT SCALE

The Instructional Development Scale consists of 26 discrete items in three subsections: Designs and Plans Instruction, Creates and Maintains a Learning Climate, Implements and Manages Instruction and Assessment.

Directions:

    a) For each scale please mark only the descriptors that were actually observed.

    b) Next, choose a level of overall proficiency for each scale.

    Level ① = Student teacher has not yet developed or used this skill.

    Level ② = Student teacher is beginning to incorporate this skill.

    Level ③ = Student teacher uses this skill appropriately.

    Level ④ = Student teacher uses this skill appropriately and consistently.

    Level ⑤ = Student teacher uses this skill appropriately and consistently, with a high degree of competence and confidence.

Note: Proficiency level does not necessarily correspond to the number of check marks given.

Designs and Plans Instruction

1) Specifies desired learner outcomes for lessons

① ② ③ ④ ⑤

- ☐ Desired learner outcome(s) described in clear and consistent terms.
- ☐ Logically sequenced.
- ☐ Appropriate to student achievement level(s).
- ☐ Directly linked to unit goals and to state/district/school standards.

Comments:

2) Specifies teaching procedures for lessons

① ② ③ ④ ⑤

- ☐ Referenced to the objective(s)/outcome(s).
- ☐ Appropriate to accomplishing objective(s)/outcome(s).
- ☐ Logically sequenced.
- ☐ Transitions are planned from one activity to another.

Comments:

3) Specifies resources for lessons

① ② ③ ④ ⑤

- ☐ Relevance to learning activity.
- ☐ Lesson plans include specific description of resources, such as title, page, equipment.
- ☐ Concrete or manipulative materials are identified when appropriate.
- ☐ Creative use of resources.

Comments:

4) Specifies procedures for assessing student progress

① ② ③ ④ ⑤

- ☐ Written lesson plans include informal assessments of student learning.
- ☐ Tests and other formal assessments focus directly on instructional goals and objectives and assess only the content that was taught.
- ☐ Develops and maintains an accurate record of student performance, e.g. grade book, anecdotal notes, test scores, portfolio.
- ☐ Considers multiple sources of assessment data when making instructional decisions.

Comments:

5) Plans for student diversity, abilities and styles

① ② ③ ④ ⑤

- ☐ Presents instruction based on assessment of student's performance.
- ☐ Provides remedial or enrichment materials/instruction when appropriate.
- ☐ Plans individual student conferences to discuss learning or motivational problems.
- ☐ Varies instructional strategies in accordance with student needs.

Comments:

6) Plans address all levels of knowledge and understanding

① ② ③ ④ ⑤

- ☐ Plans require students to memorize important vs. trivial information and to comprehend or interpret information as appropriate.
- ☐ Plans require students to apply information to real life settings.
- ☐ Plans require students to identify/clarify complex ideas or to synthesize knowledge by integrating information.
- ☐ Plans stress depth as well as breadth of content coverage.

Comments:

<table>
<tr><td>STUDENT TEACHER NAME</td><td>ID #</td><td>DATE</td></tr>
</table>

Creates and Maintains a Learning Climate

7) Communicates enthusiasm for student learning	8) Demonstrates warmth and friendliness	9) Shows sensitivity to needs and feelings of students
① ② ③ ④ ⑤	① ② ③ ④ ⑤	① ② ③ ④ ⑤

7) Communicates enthusiasm for student learning
① ② ③ ④ ⑤

- ☐ Eye contact or facial expressions communicate pleasure, concern, interest, etc.
- ☐ Voice inflections stress points of interest and importance.
- ☐ Communicates enthusiasm through movement in the classroom.
- ☐ Gestures accentuate points.

Comments:

8) Demonstrates warmth and friendliness
① ② ③ ④ ⑤

- ☐ Asks about student's interests and opinions.
- ☐ Interacts in a relaxed and informal way with students.
- ☐ Moves freely among students.
- ☐ Uses students' names in a warm and friendly way.

Comments:

9) Shows sensitivity to needs and feelings of students
① ② ③ ④ ⑤

- ☐ Students are reinforced when they do well.
- ☐ Students are encouraged when they have difficulty.
- ☐ Students' contributions are accepted in a positive manner.
- ☐ Students are treated with respect and courtesy.

Comments:

10) Provides feedback to students about behavior
① ② ③ ④ ⑤

- ☐ Student teacher clearly states expectations about appropriate behavior.
- ☐ Student teacher provides verbal feedback for acceptable behavior.
- ☐ Student teacher provides non-verbal feedback for acceptable or unacceptable behavior.
- ☐ Student teacher's language is free of derogatory references or sarcasm.

Comments:

11) Maintains positive classroom behavior
① ② ③ ④ ⑤

- ☐ Techniques that help students learn self-management and personal responsibility are utilized.
- ☐ Inconsequential behavior problems are overlooked or none exist.
- ☐ Appropriate behavior is reinforced.
- ☐ Appropriate student behaviors are maintained by maximizing opportunities for each individual to succeed.

Comments:

12) Manages disruptive behavior
① ② ③ ④ ⑤

- ☐ Individuals who have caused disruptions are dealt with rather than entire class being punished.
- ☐ Major disruptions are attended to quickly and appropriately.
- ☐ Consequences for misbehavior are based on the severity of the disruption.
- ☐ Disruptive behavior rarely occurs.

Comments:

<table>
<tr><td>STUDENT TEACHER NAME</td><td>ID #</td><td>DATE</td></tr>
</table>

Implements and Manages Instruction and Assessment

13) Begins lesson effectively

① ② ③ ④ ⑤

- ☐ Student teacher activates/establishes students' prior knowledge of current lesson.
- ☐ Student teacher helps students to understand the purpose or importance of the lesson.
- ☐ Student teacher links new information to students' existing knowledge.
- ☐ Student teacher stimulates interest in lesson by actively involving students or by asking thought-provoking questions.

Comments:

14) Presents information clearly

① ② ③ ④ ⑤

- ☐ Student teacher directly relates information to desired learner outcomes.
- ☐ Student teacher presents information in a logical sequence.
- ☐ Student teacher provides concrete and/or visual models when appropriate.
- ☐ Student teacher uses vocabulary appropriate to students' level of understanding.

Comments:

15) Gives clear directions and explanations

① ② ③ ④ ⑤

- ☐ Student teacher presents directions in a logical sequence.
- ☐ Student teacher writes critical information on board, chart or overhead.
- ☐ Student teacher clearly informs students what they should be doing, where to do it, and for how long.
- ☐ Student teacher checks students' understanding of directions before they practice independently.

Comments:

16) Uses students responses and questions in teaching

① ② ③ ④ ⑤

- ☐ Student teacher encourages students' responses and/or questions.
- ☐ Student teacher responds in a positive and supportive manner.
- ☐ Student teacher incorporates student responses and questions into the lesson.
- ☐ Student teacher uses responses to monitor student understanding of the information presented.

Comments:

17) Maximizes opportunities for all to participate

① ② ③ ④ ⑤

- ☐ Student teacher asks questions of whole group first, rather than individuals.
- ☐ Student teacher provides ample wait-time for all students after asking questions and redirects accordingly.
- ☐ Student teacher offers frequent opportunities for student-to-student interactions/inquiry.
- ☐ Student teacher provides many opportunities for covert/overt participation; physical movement, small group activities, discussions.

Comments:

18) Provides students feedback throughout lesson

① ② ③ ④ ⑤

- ☐ Student teacher provides feedback to students as soon as possible.
- ☐ Student teacher provides feedback to students in a positive manner.
- ☐ Student teacher reviews students' strengths and weaknesses and offers suggestions on how performance can be improved.
- ☐ Student teacher helps students evaluate their own performance.

Comments:

19) Promotes student retention and understanding

① ② ③ ④ ⑤

- ☐ Student teacher uses techniques which help make material relevant to students and explains the importance of the lesson.
- ☐ Student teacher defines or models the expectations of the lesson or learning.
- ☐ Student teacher provides opportunity for all students to demonstrate an understanding of what is being taught.
- ☐ Student teacher monitors student responses, interprets the source of student errors, and adjusts instruction accordingly.

Comments:

20) Uses effective closure or summarization technique

① ② ③ ④ ⑤

- ☐ Student teacher gives students an opportunity for closure/ summarization at the end of distinct segments within the lesson or between objectives.
- ☐ Student teacher provides opportunity for the student to summarize at the end of each lesson.
- ☐ Student teacher actively involves students in their own closure/summarization.
- ☐ Student teacher extends closure/summarization to future applications or actions.

Comments:

21) Uses instructional material effectively

① ② ③ ④ ⑤

- ☐ Student teacher uses instructional equipment and other aids, such as charts, graphs, overhead, video, slides, software, maps and/or manipulatives.
- ☐ Student teacher uses instructional resources that contribute to the students' understanding of lesson goals/objectives.
- ☐ Student teacher smoothly blends media with other types of instruction.
- ☐ Student teacher creates original instructional aids which are relevant and enhance the effectiveness of the teaching.

Comments:

22) Promotes individual student learning

① ② ③ ④ ⑤

- ☐ Materials chosen are directly related to the goals/objectives of the lesson.
- ☐ Materials selected ensure appropriate level of student success.
- ☐ Students are given ample opportunity to use materials as intended.
- ☐ Students' interaction with the materials is monitored to determine their level of understanding.

Comments:

23) Uses teaching methods appropriately/effectively

① ② ③ ④ ⑤

- ☐ Student teacher uses a variety of methods within the lesson: drill, inquiry, discussion, role playing, demonstration, explanation, problem-solving, cooperative learning.
- ☐ Student teacher uses method(s) that accomplish desired outcome(s).
- ☐ Student teacher adjusts instructional methods according to student progress.
- ☐ Student teacher makes smooth transitions between instructional activities within a lesson.

Comments:

24) Uses instructional time effectively

① ② ③ ④ ⑤

- ☐ Activities begin on schedule.
- ☐ Allocated instructional time is maximized.
- ☐ Instructional pacing is appropriate for students.
- ☐ There are no significant delays or periods of time during which the students are not effectively engaged.

Comments:

25) Demonstrates knowledge of subject	**26) Manages conditions for teaching and learning**
① ② ③ ④ ⑤	① ② ③ ④ ⑤
☐ Student teacher's subject area knowledge is accurate and current. ☐ Information and materials present concepts and ideas in multiple ways. ☐ Student teacher asks higher order questions and/or builds on students' questions. ☐ Student teacher is enthusiastic about content area and is able to involve or motivate students in subject matter.	☐ Basic management skills are implemented to efficiently and effectively instruct the class. Instructional tools are readily accessible. ☐ Student interactions are facilitated by room arrangements. ☐ Routine tasks are handled smoothly by teacher and/or students (attendance, lunch count, etc.). ☐ Materials and supplies are readily available. Distribution and collection of materials have been planned.
Comments:	Comments:

Must be typed.
This evaluation is to be used for employment purposes and to detail the completion of student teaching. It is intended to provide the prospective employer with specific, pertinent information regarding the student teacher's performance. The student teacher will submit the original to the Office of Professional Field Experiences for appropriate signatures and processing. It will then be the student teacher's responsibility to submit copies of this evaluation to potential employers.

STUDENT TEACHER (LAST, FIRST, MIDDLE)	SCHOOL DISTRICT	SCHOOL
CITY, STATE	MENTOR'S NAME	DATE
GRADE LEVEL(S) TAUGHT/SUBJECT	SUPERVISOR'S NAME	

Summary Narrative – please provide a brief description of classroom setting, review of student teacher's strengths, contributions and professional potential.

Student Teacher: _______________________________   Date: _____________ Page 2 of 3

PROFESSIONAL ATTRIBUTES AND CHARACTERISTICS SCALE

1. Attendance
- ☐ Frequently absent
- ☐ Rarely absent
- ☐ Exemplary attendance

2. Punctuality
- ☐ Frequently late
- ☐ Generally punctual
- ☐ Always on time

3. Professional Appearance
- ☐ Occasionally appears inappropriately/ unprofessionally dressed
- ☐ Is usually dressed appropriately
- ☐ Always dresses/appears in a professional manner

4. Oral Expression
- ☐ Makes frequent usage and/or grammatical errors
- ☐ Inarticulate
- ☐ Articulate
- ☐ Expressive, Animated

5. Written Expression
- ☐ Written work contains misspellings and/or grammatical errors
- ☐ Writing is often unclear and disorganized
- ☐ Written work is organized and clearly expresses ideas
- ☐ Uses written forms to effectively communicate with parents, administrators, and/or colleagues.

6. Tact, Judgment
- ☐ Thoughtless: insensitive to other's feelings and opinions
- ☐ Somewhat or sometimes insensitive and undiplomatic
- ☐ Perceives what to do or say in order to maintain good relations with others and responds accordingly
- ☐ Diplomatic, highly sensitive to others' feelings and opinions

7. Reliability /Dependability
- ☐ Sometimes fails to complete assigned tasks and duties
- ☐ Sometimes needs to be reminded to attend to assigned tasks and duties
- ☐ Responsible: attends to assigned tasks and duties on schedule without prompting
- ☐ Self-starter: perceives needs and attends to them immediately

8. Self-initiative/Independence
- ☐ Passive: depends on others for direction, ideas, and guidance
- ☐ Has good ideas, works effectively with limited supervision
- ☐ Creative and resourceful, independently implements plans

9. Self-Confidence
- ☐ Anxious: often appears self-conscience, nervous
- ☐ Arrogant: has unfounded belief in abilities
- ☐ Usually confident-comfortable in classroom situations
- ☐ Realistically self assured: competently handles class demands

10. Collegiality
- ☐ Prefers to work in isolation
- ☐ Reluctant to share ideas and materials
- ☐ Often participates in team efforts
- ☐ Willingly shares ideas and materials

11. Interaction with Students
- ☐ Can appear threatening or antagonistic towards students
- ☐ Shy: hesitant to work with students
- ☐ Relates easily and positively with students
- ☐ Outgoing: actively seeks opportunities to work with students

12. Response to Students' Needs
- ☐ Does not attempt to accommodate needs of unique learners
- ☐ Makes negative comments about students' ability to learn
- ☐ Usually accepts responsibility for all students' learning
- ☐ Consistently responds to learning needs of all students

13. Response to Feedback
- ☐ Defensive: unreceptive to feedback
- ☐ Receptive: but doesn't implement suggestions
- ☐ Receptive: and adjusts performance accordingly
- ☐ Eager: solicits suggestions and feedback from others

14. Ability to Reflect and Improve Performance
- ☐ Reluctant to analyze teaching performance
- ☐ Makes some effort to review teaching skills
- ☐ Actively seeks ways to assess teaching abilities
- ☐ Consistently deepens knowledge of classroom practice and students' learning

15. Professional Characteristics   S = Seldom,   U = Usually,   A = Always

S U A The Student Teacher:

- ☐☐☐ Commitment – demonstrates genuine concern for students and is dedicated to the teaching profession
- ☐☐☐ Creativity – seeks opportunities to provide unique learning experiences and develops imaginative lessons
- ☐☐☐ Flexibility – responds to unforeseen circumstances in appropriate manner and modifies actions or plans when necessary
- ☐☐☐ Integrity – maintains high ethical and professional standards and responds to district policies appropriately
- ☐☐☐ Organization – is efficient: successfully manages multiple tasks simultaneously and establishes/maintains effective classroom routines/procedures
- ☐☐☐ Perseverance – Gives best effort, strives to complete tasks and works to improve teaching skills, management strategies
- ☐☐☐ Positive Disposition – possesses pleasant interpersonal skills, is patient, resilient, optimistic and easy to approach

Student Teacher: _________________________________   Date: _____________ Page 3 of 3

Proficiency levels indicate the student teacher competency level at the end of the semester apprenticeship.
Level 1 = Student Teacher has not yet developed or used this skill.
Level 2 = Student teacher is beginning to incorporate this skill in his/her instructional repertoire.
Level 3 = Student Teacher uses this skill appropriately.
Level 4 = Student Teacher uses this skill appropriately and consistently.
Level 5 = Student Teacher uses this skill appropriately and consistently with a high degree of competence and confidence.

INSTRUCTIONAL DEVELOPMENT SCALE

Area	Proficiency 1	2	3	4	5
Designs and Plans Instruction					
1. Specifies desired learner outcomes for lessons					
2. Specifies teaching procedures for lessons					
3. Specifies resources for lessons					
4. Specifies procedures for assessing student progress					
5. Plans for student diversity, abilities and styles					
6. Plans address all levels of knowledge and understanding					
Creates and Maintains a Learning Climate					
7. Communicates enthusiasm for student learning					
8. Demonstrates warmth and friendliness					
9. Shows sensitivity to needs/feelings of students					
10. Provides feedback to students about behavior					
11. Maintains positive classroom behavior					
12. Manages disruptive behavior					

Area	Proficiency 1	2	3	4	5
Implements and Manages Instruction and Assessment					
13. Begins lesson effectively					
14. Presents information clearly					
15. Gives clear directions and explanations					
16. Uses student responses/ questions					
17. Maximizes opportunities for all to participate					
18. Provides students feedback throughout lesson					
19. Promotes student retention and understanding					
20. Uses effective closure/ summarization techniques					
21. Uses instructional material effectively					
22. Promotes individual student learning					
23. Uses teaching methods appropriately/effectively					
24. Uses instructional time effectively					
25. Demonstrates knowledge of subject					
26. Manages conditions for teaching and learning					

Summary Statement Potential as a Teacher
☐ Recommend review of career options and consideration of profession other than teaching.
☐ Recommend continuation in teaching profession
☐ Highly recommend continuation in teaching profession: strong candidate

Signature, Mentor Teacher	**Date**	**Signature, Student Teacher**	**Date**
Signature, University Supervisor	**Date**	**Checked by Professional Field Experience**	**Date**

Must be typed.

This evaluation is to be used for employment purposes and to detail the completion of student teaching. It is intended to provide the prospective employer with specific, pertinent information regarding the student teacher's performance. The student teacher will submit the original to the Office of Professional Field Experiences for appropriate signatures and processing. It will then be the student teacher's responsibility to submit copies of this evaluation to potential employers.

STUDENT TEACHER (LAST, FIRST, MIDDLE)	SCHOOL DISTRICT	SCHOOL
CITY, STATE	MENTOR'S NAME	DATE
GRADE LEVEL(S) TAUGHT/SUBJECT	SUPERVISOR'S NAME	

Summary Narrative – please provide a brief description of classroom setting, review of student teacher's strengths, contributions and professional potential.

Student Teacher: _________________________________   Date: ______________ Page 2 of 3

PROFESSIONAL ATTRIBUTES AND CHARACTERISTICS SCALE

1. Attendance ☐ Frequently absent ☐ Rarely absent ☐ Exemplary attendance	**2. Punctuality** ☐ Frequently late ☐ Generally punctual ☐ Always on time	**3. Professional Appearance** ☐ Occasionally appears inappropriately/ unprofessionally dressed ☐ Is usually dressed appropriately ☐ Always dresses/appears in a professional manner
4. Oral Expression ☐ Makes frequent usage and/or grammatical errors ☐ Inarticulate ☐ Articulate ☐ Expressive, Animated	**5. Written Expression** ☐ Written work contains misspellings and/or grammatical errors ☐ Writing is often unclear and disorganized ☐ Written work is organized and clearly expresses ideas ☐ Uses written forms to effectively communicate with parents, administrators, and/or colleagues.	**6. Tact, Judgment** ☐ Thoughtless: insensitive to other's feelings and opinions ☐ Somewhat or sometimes insensitive and undiplomatic ☐ Perceives what to do or say in order to maintain good relations with others and responds accordingly ☐ Diplomatic, highly sensitive to others' feelings and opinions
7. Reliability /Dependability ☐ Sometimes fails to complete assigned tasks and duties ☐ Sometimes needs to be reminded to attend to assigned tasks and duties ☐ Responsible: attends to assigned tasks and duties on schedule without prompting ☐ Self-starter: perceives needs and attends to them immediately	**8. Self-initiative/Independence** ☐ Passive: depends on others for direction, ideas, and guidance ☐ Has good ideas, works effectively with limited supervision ☐ Creative and resourceful, independently implements plans	**9. Self-Confidence** ☐ Anxious: often appears self-conscience, nervous ☐ Arrogant: has unfounded belief in abilities ☐ Usually confident-comfortable in classroom situations ☐ Realistically self assured: competently handles class demands
10. Collegiality ☐ Prefers to work in isolation ☐ Reluctant to share ideas and materials ☐ Often participates in team efforts ☐ Willingly shares ideas and materials	**11. Interaction with Students** ☐ Can appear threatening or antagonistic towards students ☐ Shy: hesitant to work with students ☐ Relates easily and positively with students ☐ Outgoing: actively seeks opportunities to work with students	**12. Response to Students' Needs** ☐ Does not attempt to accommodate needs of unique learners ☐ Makes negative comments about students' ability to learn ☐ Usually accepts responsibility for all students' learning ☐ Consistently responds to learning needs of all students

13. Response to Feedback ☐ Defensive: unreceptive to feedback ☐ Receptive: but doesn't implement suggestions ☐ Receptive: and adjusts performance accordingly ☐ Eager: solicits suggestions and feedback from others	**14. Ability to Reflect and Improve Performance** ☐ Reluctant to analyze teaching performance ☐ Makes some effort to review teaching skills ☐ Actively seeks ways to assess teaching abilities ☐ Consistently deepens knowledge of classroom practice and students' learning

15. Professional Characteristics   S = Seldom,   U = Usually,   A = Always

S U A The Student Teacher:

☐☐☐ Commitment – demonstrates genuine concern for students and is dedicated to the teaching profession

☐☐☐ Creativity – seeks opportunities to provide unique learning experiences and develops imaginative lessons

☐☐☐ Flexibility – responds to unforeseen circumstances in appropriate manner and modifies actions or plans when necessary

☐☐☐ Integrity – maintains high ethical and professional standards and responds to district policies appropriately

☐☐☐ Organization – is efficient: successfully manages multiple tasks simultaneously and establishes/maintains effective classroom routines/procedures

☐☐☐ Perseverance – Gives best effort, strives to complete tasks and works to improve teaching skills, management strategies

☐☐☐ Positive Disposition – possesses pleasant interpersonal skills, is patient, resilient, optimistic and easy to approach

Student Teacher: _________________________________   Date: _____________ Page 3 of 3

Proficiency levels indicate the student teacher competency level at the end of the semester apprenticeship.
Level 1 = Student Teacher has not yet developed or used this skill.
Level 2 = Student teacher is beginning to incorporate this skill in his/her instructional repertoire.
Level 3 = Student Teacher uses this skill appropriately.
Level 4 = Student Teacher uses this skill appropriately and consistently.
Level 5 = Student Teacher uses this skill appropriately and consistently with a high degree of competence and confidence.

INSTRUCTIONAL DEVELOPMENT SCALE

Area	Proficiency 1	2	3	4	5
Designs and Plans Instruction					
1. Specifies desired learner outcomes for lessons					
2. Specifies teaching procedures for lessons					
3. Specifies resources for lessons					
4. Specifies procedures for assessing student progress					
5. Plans for student diversity, abilities and styles					
6. Plans address all levels of knowledge and understanding					
Creates and Maintains a Learning Climate					
7. Communicates enthusiasm for student learning					
8. Demonstrates warmth and friendliness					
9. Shows sensitivity to needs/feelings of students					
10. Provides feedback to students about behavior					
11. Maintains positive classroom behavior					
12. Manages disruptive behavior					

Area	Proficiency 1	2	3	4	5
Implements and Manages Instruction and Assessment					
13. Begins lesson effectively					
14. Presents information clearly					
15. Gives clear directions and explanations					
16. Uses student responses/ questions					
17. Maximizes opportunities for all to participate					
18. Provides students feedback throughout lesson					
19. Promotes student retention and understanding					
20. Uses effective closure/ summarization techniques					
21. Uses instructional material effectively					
22. Promotes individual student learning					
23. Uses teaching methods appropriately/effectively					
24. Uses instructional time effectively					
25. Demonstrates knowledge of subject					
26. Manages conditions for teaching and learning					

Summary Statement Potential as a Teacher
☐ Recommend review of career options and consideration of profession other than teaching.
☐ Recommend continuation in teaching profession
☐ Highly recommend continuation in teaching profession: strong candidate

Signature, Mentor Teacher	Date	Signature, Student Teacher	Date
Signature, University Supervisor	Date	Checked by Professional Field Experience	Date

UNIVERSITY SUPERVISOR EVALUATION: STUDENT TEACHER PRESPECTIVE
8-Week Experience

Supervisor's Name _________________________________ Date ____________

	Not applicable	1 = least satisfied			5 = most satisfied	

SUPPORT/COMMUNICATION

	Not applicable	1	2	3	4	5
a. Advised/reviewed student teaching requirements at the beginning of the semester	X	1	2	3	4	5
b. Was accessible by phone and/or e-mail	X	1	2	3	4	5
c. Responded to my messages in a timely manner	X	1	2	3	4	5
d. Provided useful information through seminars, workshops, counseling, etc.	X	1	2	3	4	5
e. Reviewed timecard, notebook and weekly entries	X	1	2	3	4	5
f. Discussed lesson plan requirements	X	1	2	3	4	5
g. If difficulties occurred, helped to provide a workable solution	X	1	2	3	4	5

SUPERVISION/ASSESSMENT

	Not applicable	1	2	3	4	5
h. Observed me a minimum of 1 time	X	1	2	3	4	5
i. Visited me a minimum of 2 times	X	1	2	3	4	5
j. Spent ample time (30-60) min) for observation/assessment	X	1	2	3	4	5
k. Analyzed and critiqued my teaching technique soon after each observation	X	1	2	3	4	5
l. Helped me identify specific areas of strength and weakness	X	1	2	3	4	5
m. Previewed and discussed the purposes of each evaluation form	X	1	2	3	4	5
n. Reviewed the results of each evaluation with me	X	1	2	3	4	5
o. conducted a three-way conference with student teacher and cooperating teacher	X	1	2	3	4	5
p. Conferences were conducted in a positive and constructive manner	X	1	2	3	4	5

Comments:

____

____